Resources for Reading;
Does Quality Count?

LI HE

Resources for Reading; Does Quality Count?

Proceedings of the Twenty-Second Annual Course and
Conference of the United Kingdom Reading
Association,
University of Reading, July 1985

Editor: Betty Root

M
MACMILLAN

First published 1986

Published by
MACMILLAN EDUCATION LTD
Houndmills, Basingstoke, Hampshire RG21 2XS
and London
Companies and representatives
throughout the world

Typeset by Wessex Typesetters
(Division of The Eastern Press Ltd)
Frome, Somerset

Printed in Great Britain by
Anchor Brendon Ltd,
Tiptree, Essex

ISBN 0–333–417739

Contents

Acknowledgements

Titch by Pat Hutchins is reproduced by kind permission of The Bodley Head; and the extract from *Writing: Teachers and Children at Work* is reproduced by kind permission of Heinemann Educational Books, Inc.

The editor, Betty Root, would like to express her sincere thanks to Bridie Raban, who so generously helped with the editing of the proceeding.

Introduction

The theme of the UKRA Conference 1985, held in the University of Reading, was 'Resources for Reading; Does Quality Count?' Many people generously contributed time and expertise to present a variety of stimulating papers in plenary sessions, key lectures and workshops. All were enthusiastically received by energetic and dedicated conference delegates.

Regretably, it is not possible or necessarily advisable to represent all thirty-five contributors in this collection of papers. From those received I have attempted to make a selection which reflects the theme I chose for this particular conference. The focus on the quality of resources is a deliberate attempt to try and assess the importance of the books, materials and methods used every day in our schools.

Whilst the old adage that a good teacher can make the most banal reading text interesting, remains to some extent true, it has in the past encouraged complacency. Well-presented and researched resources should, in time, lift the quality of teaching and, in consequence, of learning. No one doubts the difficulty of effecting change in the classroom but there are indications, observed by those closely associated with in-service activities, that this factor is beginning to surface in many schools.

The responsibility to ensure that this continues must be shared by teachers and publishers working together towards a common aim – helping children to read and to become readers.

Betty Root

Part I

Implications for the Content of Reading

Chapter 1

In Defence of Reading Schemes

Betty Root

This brief paper attempts to remind readers that those responsible for in-service and initial training should, at all times, ensure that their own points of view are tempered with tolerance. Education needs enthusiasts and in the field of helping children to read there will always be divergent opinions. In expressing them we should all aim to build confidence, not destroy it. Teachers are responsible for their own choice and need constructive help to enable them to decide with is the best way for them.

It is paradoxical that the more we understand the reading process the less certain many teachers become about what they should be doing to help young children learn to read. If politicians yearn for the return of Victorian virtues there must similarly be times when teachers could be justified in looking back to those days when simplistic notions about the theories of reading prevailed and choice was almost non-existent. Diversions along the narrow path were positively discouraged, for the teaching of reading was perceived as a science composed of slowly-accumulated facts.

During the past two decades issues have certainly grown more complex and the choices have multiplied. It would be foolish to pretend that a clear sense of direction has been established but there seems to be emerging yet another crossroad where teachers are being overwhelmed with arguments concerning the choice between using a published reading programme or relegating all such books to the boiler room. This appears to have replaced the dilemma of earlier years between teaching phonics or look and say (some people will say this problem has not been solved!). The teaching of reading has always created a loony left and a loony right.

Currently the 'experts' are intent on causing confusion and disruption and in so doing all they are achieving is an undermining of teachers' confidence. It is relatively easy to write lucidly in a textbook about the virtues of using only 'good children's literature' in the early stages of reading. Such writers reveal a certain arrogance concerning their judgement of what constitutes a 'good' book. And such writers have almost certainly not been exposed to the unremitting daily pressures exerted by a class of mixed-ability lively children. It is totally irresponsible to denigrate teaching techniques which invariably have been found to achieve the required goals.

In any case, it would be naïve for anyone to assume that in reality teachers find themselves with such limited options. For they have always had the wisdom to appreciate that different children need different help at different times. Teachers do need to be conversant with all the alternatives and those with the authority to disseminate this knowledge should extend a greater sense of tolerance and not put forward only one rigid point of view.

Because some teachers may choose to use a published reading programme to act as a spine or a core to their overall language policy, this does not indicate that their children are deprived of the wealth of stories, poems and information books which exist outside structured schemes. Neither should it imply that the books within schemes have nothing to offer.

In the immediate post-war years the idea of a carefully controlled vocabulary flourished and, understandably, schemes perpetually became associated with boring, repetitive, meaningless prose. As vehicles of meaning these schemes were undoubtedly a complete failure; as stimulants to literacy they were disastrous. Reading was a task to be endured, not enjoyed. The following extracts confirm this:

> Daddy is a nice man.
> Mummy is nice too.   (*Topsy and Sam*) Cassell
>
> Bring the pot Ann for the cod.   (*Radiant Way*)
>   W. R. Chambers
>
> Dick said 'Look, look. Look up
>   Look up, up up.'   (*Happy Trio*) Wheaton

Mum met ten men in Pat's tent.　　　(*Words in Colour*)
　　　　　　　　　　　　　　　　　　Cuisenhaire

Understandably, there has persisted in the field of primary education an insistence that all reading schemes are still devoid of literary merit. What nonsense! *Breakthrough to Literacy*, published by Longman in 1970 was one of the earlier examples of a new image. Since its publication an increasing number of respected and acclaimed childrens' authors have joined forces with experienced teachers and responsible publishers to produce thoughtful and sensitively-written schemes. The discreet structure contained in them, which is so essential to some children's learning, is not easy to achieve. Restricting the input of new words, constructing sentences so that difficult vocabulary can be guessed in context, creating familiar characters to give more meaning and depth to the story – all these are constraints which many authors absorb into their writing with imagination and ingenuity. Not a few teachers are grateful for their expertise because they recognise that in the early stages of learning to read what matters above all else is for the children to succeed. Failure, even at the most superficial level, can so quickly effect a child's attitude to reading. Teachers know that they need to manipulate the situation to avoid a loss of confidence and well-designed schemes are supportive to children in their first tentative efforts to read.

It is fully accepted that there are children who seem to acquire a knowledge of reading by osmosis, often absorbing the process before formal schooling. But you would need a great deal of courage to assume that all children learn in this way provided they are read to frequently and surrounded by beautiful books. Where is the research to suggest this is a possibility?

There is no evidence to show that reading schemes are disappearing from primary schools, and publishers are obviously optimistic that teachers will still be looking for fresh resources into the next decade. The most promising change is that very few schools rely solely on one basic programme. Teachers are insisting on the availability of a selection of schemes to provide a choice for the children and for themselves.

All the arguments for the retention of a published reading

programme rests on one significant factor. It is, of course, concerned with the quality of the stories in the books. Although the abject poverty of most earlier reading books has already been illustrated, not all of them fall into this category. The Beacon Reading Scheme (1922) was very forward looking in its day, even saying in the handbook, in connection with attacking new words, that children should be encouraged 'to make that good and legitimate use of the context as a guide to word recognition which the adult makes'. Some of the books from the upper levels survive to this day simply because their literary content remains superior to many subsequent competitors. 'Peter and Jane' will surely not be with us in the twenty-first century to dull our senses!

Nearly all the schemes published before 1970 revealed little or no evidence that teachers and children had been consulted during the schemes' development. Sadly, the disappearance of almost all these books has not totally eliminated the rubbish, but this will always be so. More sophisticated production methods and the wide use of full-colour, glossy covers can still mask the mundane text. But there is cause for optimism if you look carefully at any present-day extensive exhibition of reading books.

Publishers frequently undertake the responsibility of sifting research findings, and contemporary reading programmes, in some instances, do reflect trends in educational thinking. Published material in itself can sometimes point the way to new methods and changed attitudes.

Teachers are responsible for their own choice and most have the opportunity for flexibility within their classrooms. Whilst the needs of individual children takes precedence over all else, this requires a carefully planned programme with a clear view ahead. Guidance along a pathway to success may certainly be facilitated by the use of reading schemes or teachers may successfully bring together other resources. Whichever way is taken the books available in our schools and homes should, through the excitement and fascination of stories, poems and facts, give children the rewards they need to become competent and willing readers. And once they have achieved this goal we need to allow time for them to relish this absorbing pleasure.

Chapter 2

The Quality of Story

Ralph Lavender

All human beings need to make narratives, and narratives in word language are, because of their special relationship to learning to read, the true context for the teaching of reading. Some of the qualities of stories are described − of entertainment, of developing language, of the growth of compassion, of imagery, of emotional experience and of hypothetical thinking. It is suggested that these qualities relate significantly to a reader's growing tolerance of ambiguity. Stories teach living as well as reading.

Narrative imagination and reading

In planning this paper on the quality of resources for reading in relation to stories and books for children, it seemed sensible to begin by going to the children, who are, after all, the consumers of reading schemes, but who in the past have been allowed little say in the matter. It is a mark of a good school that the children have a stake in their destiny as learners. It's Melanie who comes to my aid: she was six when I asked her what stories are about; and her answer was 'Rabbits. And rainbows sometimes.'

I must first say that I've never been able to find a child who couldn't tell me a story. Such children may exist, but I have not discovered them. I shall be trying to show that children do all they need to do with a story right from the beginning; it's something we don't need to teach them. If I am right, certain implications must follow for how we go about teaching reading, because if, like all good teachers, we wish to start from where the children are, and stories are where *they* are, then that's where we should start. Barbara Hardy (1975, p. vii) tells us that 'nature, not art, makes us all storytellers . . . Narrative imagination is a common human possession.' It may be true that as adults we tell fewer stories than when we were children: for us, there are our dreams; and the tales told post-interview and post-traffic accident, when we did not do as well as we would like to have done. It may also be true that children are better at 'storying', as it has been called, provided nobody has suggested to them that telling stories equals telling lies.

So I asked Melanie to tell me a story. She had already said that 'Rapunzel' was her favourite story. Here, then, is her story:

> Once upon a time there was a rabbit, and a daddy rabbit, and a mummy rabbit, and the queen rabbit, she, she was the best rabbit of all of them. One day, a witch rabbit came by, and the witch took the princess rabbit away, and the princess rabbit, when she made a ladder, and she climbed down from where she was staying, where the witch had put her, and she went back to her mother, and one day when she was going out she met a prince, and they got married.

It will be noted that Melanie has retold 'Rapunzel' for rabbits. She has done some other interesting and important things, as well, in terms of language and the organisation of her thinking, but they're outside the scope of my paper. Like all traditional tales – myths, legends, folk-tales and fairy stories, all encompassed in the Norse culture by the single word 'saga' – 'Rapunzel' contains essential psychic, even phallic material as Bruno Bettelheim (1976) says. In such stories, there is much useful sinning to be done from a safe distance: Midas, Loki, and Rama and Sita attest to this. Some of it takes place through the guise of animals, such as the Brer Rabbits and the Anansis of this world, and there can be no safer distance than that. In stories for young children, and in many traditional tales, the child's longing for an ordered universe is answered, where the rules are most powerfully demonstrated by the exceptions. In such tales, ordinary people – the poor, the weak, the hungry and the oppressed – are transfigured at extraordinary moments in their lives. At this stage for the child, then, good morality, which means the punishment of the wolf in 'The Three Little Pigs' by being boiled alive, is even preferable to good literary quality. Indeed, without a villain, there is no story: if there's no fox, 'Rosie's Walk' (Hutchins, 1970) doesn't exist; nothing much would have happened to Edmund, Lucy and the others, without the White Witch.

Ambiguity

Sinning at a safe distance is one of the things we do most valuably in story and poem. Death is the only other sin we are all obliged to commit, and there are many fine stories for children that approach this fact of existence with both sensitivity and imagination. Alan Garner (1977) approaches it in his own unique way in *Tom Fobble's Day*. It is not an easy text, the writer does not tell us everything, there are tell-tale gaps for the reader to work upon – what Roland Barthes (1975) means by the reader as 'producer of text'. The child becomes an author through the act of reading. Story teaches the child how to become a reader, and this is true of Alan Garner's text no less than of the stories by Pat Hutchins and Shirley Hughes.

Garner's story, with its aspirations to the visual and the tactile (by the way, his *The Stone Book* (Garner, 1976) has the same rating on the Fry Readability Graph as *The Very Hungry Caterpillar* (Carle, 1974), a colleague once told me), is highly ambiguous. The ambiguity of Long John silver, of the plot in *Z for Zachariah* (O'Brien, 1976), and children's growing tolerance of this ambiguity should tell us how to plan our provision of literature in order to provide our children with quality. Inexperienced readers need all the answers; experienced readers bring unresolved business to their reading; and even more mature ones leave some matters still unresolved afterwards. What did Robert O'Brien's man in the orange suit intend? Less mature readers get too close, projecting themselves into a character or an event such as the death of William's grandfather, seeing the part but not the whole. More mature readers keep their distance so as to see the whole as well. The educative power of ambiguity is something we cannot shirk. In 'The Wolf and the Seven Little Kids', the big bad wolf richly deserves his fate – villains are always easily identifiable, and nothing less than capital punishment will do. Founded upon this perception are later, more complex moral judgements, like those of Ursula le Guin (1971) and the 'morality of displacement' as it has been called – the notion that one man's flood is another's drought, and that every act achieves an equal and opposite effect somewhere else.

Educating the emotions

A matter of ever-increasing importance, so I believe, is how we can help children to learn to live with their emotions and to make constructive use of them, so that they do not become, as Barbara Dockar-Drysdale (1968) says, 'frozen children' like Kay in Hans Andersen's *The Snow Queen*. Interestingly, we don't find much about this in *The Curriculum from 5 to 16* (HMSO, 1985), and it doesn't appear to be an official objective for education. Yet consider now the power of Charles Causley's poem 'Mary Mary Magdalene' (*Collected Poems*, 1975):

> Mary, Mary Magdalene
> Lying on the wall,
> I throw a pebble on your back,
> Will it lie or fall?
>
> Send me down for Christmas
> Some stockings and some hose,
> And send before the winter's end
> A brand-new suit of clothes.
>
> Mary, Mary Magdalene
> Under a stony tree,
> I throw a pebble on your back.
> What will you send me?
>
> > I'll send you for your christening
> > A woollen robe to wear,
> > A shiny cup from which to sup,
> > And a name to bear.
>
> Mary, Mary Magdalene
> Lying cool as snow,
> What will you be sending me
> When to school I go?

I'll send a pencil and a pen
That write both clean and neat,
And I'll send to the schoolmaster
A tongue that's kind and sweet.

Mary, Mary Magdalene
Lying in the sun,
What will you be sending me
Now I'm twenty-one?

I'll send you down a locket
As silver as your skin,
And I'll send you a lover
To fit a gold key in.

Mary, Mary Magdalene
Underneath the spray,
What will you be sending me
On my wedding-day?

I'll send you down some blossom,
Some ribbons and some lace,
And for the bride a veil to hide
The blushes on her face.

Mary, Mary Magdalene
Whiter than the swan,
Tell me what you'll send me,
Now my good man's dead and gone.

I'll send to you a single bed
On which you must lie,
And pillows bright where tears may light
That fall from your eye.

Mary, Mary Magdalene
Now nine months are done,
What will you be sending me
For my little son?

I'll send you for your baby
A lucky stone, and small,
To throw to Mary Magdalene
Lying on the wall.

Charles Causley: Collected Poems 1951–1975
(Macmillan, London, 1975)

Children will need to understand other people – the Steerforths and Uriah Heaps and Huck Finns of this world, and the motives for their actions, and they will need to feel compassion. Kornei Chukovsky, the Russian folklorist, had this to say in *From Two to Five* (1915, p. 138) about the goal of the storyteller:

> [it] consists of fostering in the child, at whatever cost, compassion and humaneness – this miraculous ability of man to be disturbed by another being's misfortunes, to feel joy about another's being's happiness, to experience another's fate as one's own . . . our only goal is to awaken, nurture and strengthen in the responsive soul of the child this invaluable ability to feel compassion for another's unhappiness and to share in another's happiness. Without this a man is inhuman.

We see this happening through many, many stories, both simple and complex, from *My Grandson Lew* (Zolotow, 1974) to Oscar Wilde's *The Selfish Giant* and the works of Philippa Pearce. For example, Kate in *The Way to Sattin Shore* (1984) quarrels with her brother at that point in the story where she first meets her father, without knowing him. The burden of emotion is too great for both of them; yet for the reader to understand what is hidden from the characters is to know compassion for them.

In story, we can be greedy for other people's lives. Good fantasy, of course, must incorporate aspects of the real world, be it a wardrobe, or the static electricity in *Elidor* (Garner, 1965). 'Once upon a time, a bad Weetabix went for a walk down the road', wrote a child, illustrating the same point. This confusion of conventions becomes transformed in a piece by Janet, who was eleven when she wrote:

> The quintain stood lifeless in the middle of the courtyard. Jo the cook's girl (the image of a boy) stood at one end of the courtyard stroking Jamier the tilting horse. Jo and Jamier were very good friends. All of a sudden she put down her bowl (she was peeling onions) and backed Jamier out of the stable. She was going to get a belting for being late but what did she care. She put a blanket onto Jamier's back. All at once she found herself (unwillingly)

charging at the quintain. She imagined crowds of people shouting for her and in her dreams she saw King John himself calling for her to win. BANG. She hit the quintain. 'Wait wait,' called a voice, 'you're just the boy I need,' for you remember she looked like a boy. This man (who Jo was soon to learn was Mr Poffliffe) signed Jo up for a jousting competition that afternoon, King John himself would be there. So Jo appeared at a jousting competition (with Jamier) and won and King John presented Jo with her prize which was a white linen surcoat. She didnt have to imagine anymore for this was the real thing.

It can be seen here how Janet's imagination has been fuelled by the discipline of her own intensely personal experiences.

The roots of reading and imagery

In the late 1950s, when I had just started teaching in the East End of London, a remarkable revolution in children's book publishing began to take place, largely in this country, and with writers like Rosemary Sutcliff and Geoffrey Trease. Yet it almost passed schools by, because the attention of teachers had been diverted into passionate arguments about the pedagogy of reading instruction. The result of this was that we got bogged down in the 'sentence hash' of many reading primers, which was noted by E. B. Huey (1908) and which can still be seen in some of the pasteurised books published in our own day. How much evil and how many jokes can we still find in these books?

More recently, we have come to know how essential it is that, if we care about children learning to read, we must care about the quality of what we make available for them to read. We must care about how we make books open to them. We must care about how we enable them to enter books emotionally; since the only limit to what children can take from literature is emotional. Equally, we must care about being readers of quality ourselves, since teaching children to read is perhaps the most intimate thing we do with them, and the first thing we teach them is ourselves.

And so, at last, learning to read has been really rejoined to its roots, which grow luxuriantly in the rich humus of story. Working with real books of real quality right from the very beginning might also reduce the disparity between what children choose and what their teachers would choose for them, enabling them to reach yet further in their reading. Cliff Moon's work has been tremendously influential here, and UKRA has, over the years, been paying closer and closer attention to the quality of children's fiction. Two more recent developments have been the rediscovery of parents as partners in children learning to read; and the phenomenal growth of school bookshops. We might note, in passing, that of the £90 million spent on books by schools last year, according to the Educational Publishers' Council, a quarter of it came from parents. And we might also note that one local authority proposes to buy no fiction for its public libraries this year, because it is a 'luxury'. How long will it be before bread and water become liable to VAT?

I only wish that the same critical acumen I have noted could now be applied to the illumination of children's information books. As an erstwhile judge of the *Times Educational Supplement*'s Junior Information Book Award, I am sad to see how little improvement there has been in this field. In fourteen years, the award has actually had to be withheld three times. We might also note that the narrative information book, a species, publishers tell me, that doesn't sell well, stands at the 'interface' between narrative and information. This is one place where there's much work for us all still to do.

Truth lies in the imagery, not in the characters or in the events of a story. And this is also the case for information books. It is why much more needs to be done in schools to develop children's grasp of figurative language, which neither Enid Blyton nor television make very much use of, because they don't need it. The power of the image, as Ted Hughes (1970) has observed, exists because images can migrate from their original striking places in a fashion that's beyond calculation. It is Jacques Barzun (1971) who remarks that 'the facts never speak for themselves. They must be given voice. The expression is the knowledge.' Richard Mabey (1976), writing in *Street Flowers* about the hairy bittercress, uses imagery as a means to understanding, and we begin to see how one writer can find simple words to say something complex, whilst others may use many words for something quite simple. So literature and information books of quality give us images with which to think.

Other qualities of story

Entertainment and pleasure are the first power that stories of quality can exert over all of us. We have *The Shrinking of Treehorn* by F. P. Heide (1975); we have David Jackson in 'Irritating Sayings' from an anthology called *Ways of Talking* (1978); we have the rhythms and the repetitions of Charles Causley's 'I Saw a Jolly Hunter' (*Collected Poems*, 1975), which has a point to make, too. But if stories and poems were to exist solely for their value as entertainment, they would constitute little more than chewing-gum for the mind. Even the savouring of words, as in the version of *The Sorcerer's Apprentice* (Hazen, 1971) illustrated by Tomi Ungerer, is not enough. We can feel these alliterations under our toenails, we can invest in a word like 'alantir' for a future when Tolkien may be found. The language development which can take place from such encounters is comparable to that which flows from nursery rhymes – the faded pop songs of the past. But none of this is enough to explain why we need stories.

One story contains the seed of the next, as Harold Rosen (1984) reminds us. Yet, according to Northrop Frye (1957), there is only one story, and every story is a version of that one great story, which is about losing, and finding again, personal identity. That is why so many stories demand difficult journeys be made. Frye also says that reality is what we create rather than what we contemplate; and similarly, the psychologist Richard Gregory (1974) remarks that 'we may live more by fiction than by fact'. After all, 'Dallas' and Ethiopia as we see them on our silver screens challenge our grip on reality.

Narrative and thought

Stories of all kinds are a form of hypothetical thinking. When we experience a story, we accept the author's invitation to enter an alternative world, we choose how much or how little of his characters and their histories we wish to try on in play – and, of course, children know that play, like story, is very serious business indeed. The Arabian stories of a thousand and one nights tell us that the ability to tell stories is a matter of life or death. In responding to stories, we form hypotheses about them from the evidence given. Perhaps Stig was in a plane crash, and his parents were killed, and he never heard anybody speaking . . . maybe the man in the orange suit in *Z for Zachariah* will destroy the girl . . . the stupid wolf might pull it off and catch clever Polly . . . perhaps Max did deserve to be sent to bed without any supper . . . Peter Rabbit, maybe, will get caught by Mr MacGregor.

Frank Smith (1975) told us that testing cognitive hypotheses is the basic learning process we all employ. We have no other way of learning. Science is based upon observation and hypothesis no less than is narrative: the difference lies in the nature of the data. It was Chukovsky, again, who noted that if you do not tell children fairy stories, they will simply make up their own, which suggests that such stories contain essential hypotheses. I must stress this point again: story is, like science, a way of supposing, forming a set of hypotheses about such and such a person in such and such circumstances taken to their logical conclusion – as Ivan Southall (1968) does in *Let the Balloon Go*, for example. Both are a game in the pursuit of understanding. But story goes further: it consists of imaginative transformations of reality, glimpses in advance of what might be, enabling the child to become, in Vygotsky's (1934) memorable phrase, 'a head taller than himself'.

Story is also for validating personal experience, enabling children to see themselves in a new light, giving them the shock of finding themselves in a book and realising that the author knew them all along. The earliest stories are 'transitional objects' as Winnicott (1971) called them; and there are stories about that, too, like *Dogger* by Shirley Hughes (1977), helping the child to distinguish between 'I' and 'Not-I'. Only in stories can children be truly free: for in real life, they have to be where they're put, eat what they're given, wear what they're told. Is this the root of Enid Blyton's popularity?

Narrative is virtual experience of a secondary or alternative world, enabling children to confirm and extend their understanding of reality. Being 'spectator language' as Britton (1970) calls it, narrative doesn't require us to do anything. Therefore, we are in a better position to use it as a way of finding a harmony between in-here and out-there, between inner necessities and external demands. Story lays hold of the sense of reality, and we can begin to talk about the characters as if we could know them. Isaac Bashevis Singer has said that stories are for forgetting human disasters for a while. I should want, therefore, to gloss Barbara Hardy's statement, by saying that it is neither nature nor art, but necessity that makes us all storytellers. Story is a power to be possessed: and to possess any given story is also to possess power over time. Margaret Spencer (1984) shows how narrative time is now, as you read the story, yet never, and yet always. To re-enter the narrative time, all you have to do is to read the story again.

Narrative and response

Telling a story is one of the most important ways of talking about it. It's a kind of response. Talking about stories is necessary in order to discover possibilities outside our own nomal range of response, by sharing in other people's. But if the talking is forced, then the response goes underground. If the only thing we can do is to ask factual questions of children about the stories they know and that we introduce them to – for example, about the colour of the chihuahua Ben so earnestly desires in Philippa Pearce's *A Dog so Small* (1970) – maybe it would be better to ask nothing. And then read more stories instead. Edward Blishen in a rare moment of frustration, perhaps, once spoke of 'the operating table of comprehension'.

A recent HMI survey of top junior and third-year secondary children in Rochdale showed that some children thought the statement 'I wish there were more books about . . .' was already complete. Well, at a time when there is very little in education to laugh about, this must be good news. We are all afflicted by this neurosis of evaluation. We inflict it upon ourselves, like dervishes, because we have lost our self-confidence. And it is inflicted upon us from outside by our masters. To what extent this might be a diversionary tactic, like a bankrupt attacking the insolvency of all his friends, is not for me to say. But you'll all remember the distinction Dickens drew in *Hard Times* (1854) between Gradgrind and something else that was based on 'the subtle essences of humanity', as he called them. It behoves us all to remember that, after all, facts are nothing more than stories about the evidence.

The importance of narrative and the arts

But what I can and do say is that the arts penetrate the consciousness of each one of us in a subtle, mysterious, personal manner, communicating experience in such a way as to enable us to grasp it and make sense of it. What a pity, therefore, that the objectives in *English from 5 to 16* (HMSO, 1984) only appear to admit the instrumental uses of language; and that *The Curriculum from 5 to 16* places literature with literacy rather than with aesthetics.

The effect of literature is not examinable. No set of rules fully explains, and no set of strategies enables any of us fully to learn, the richness of language – the feeling that lies in an utterance, the connotations of the words, their associations and the shadows playing between them, the resonances and the ambiguities. When the rational and the affective are in conflict, it is the affective that wins, because it is the affective that gives the power to our lives. All this is true, of course, not just for narrative in the language of words. It is equally true for other kinds of narrative – in the language of music, in the language of visual imagery, in the language of the human body, and so on. It just happens that narrative in the language of words is specially placed because of its association with learning to read.

What we need now is to rediscover our faith in ourselves as teachers, and faith in our children as learners. This evaluation neurosis undermines that faith. Professor Mary Warnock, in her Dimbleby lecture, made the crucial point that only by believing anything is possible for our children, can we achieve that which is worthwhile. What we should be concerned about above all is enabling our children to come to know what Martin

Buber (1971) called 'the heavenly bread of self-being', to be moved by their own humanity and by other people's. Stories tell us of this, too. Hans Andersen, of whom it was said that 'only a writer who can write for man is fit to write for children', wrote a little-known story called *The Most Incredible* (Haugaard, 1974) to say precisely this. And it was J. R. R. Tolkien (1964) who spoke of the 'eucatastrophe' – the literary experience that washes the soul clean.

So I come to a poem for ourselves. It was written by a Canadian boy of fourteen. He wrote for himself, as you will see, but it's as if he were speaking to us. He called it 'He Always':

He always.
He always wanted to explain things, but no one cared,
So he drew.

Sometimes he would just draw and it wasn't anything.
He wanted to carve it in stone or write it in the sky.
He would lie out on the grass and look up in the sky and it
would be only the sky and the things inside him that
needed saying.

And it was after that that he drew the picture.
It was a beautiful picture. He kept it under his pillow and
would let no one see it.
And he would look at it every night and think about it.
And when it was dark and his eyes were closed he could see
it still,
And it was all of him and he loved it.

When he started school he brought it with him,
Not to show anyone, but just to have it with him like a
friend.

It was funny about school.
He sat in a square brown desk like all the other square
desks, and he thought it would be red.
And his room was a square brown room like all the other
rooms.
And it was tight and close. And stiff.

He hated to hold the pencil and chalk, with his arms stiff
and his feet flat on the floor, stiff with the teacher
watching and watching.
The teacher came and spoke to him.
She told him to wear a tie like all the other boys.
He said he didn't like them and she said it didn't matter.

After that they drew. And he drew all yellow and it was the
way he felt about the morning.
And it was beautiful.

The teacher came and smiled at him.
'What's this?' she said. 'Why don't you draw something
like Ken's drawing?
Isn't it beautiful?'
After that his mother bought him a tie and he always drew
airplanes and rocket ships like everyone else.

And he threw the old picture away.

And when he lay out alone looking at the sky, it was big
and blue and all of everything, but he wasn't
anymore.

He was square and brown inside and his hands were stiff.
And he was like everyone else. All the things inside him
that needed saying didn't need it anymore.
It had stopped pushing. It was crushed.
Stiff.

Like everything else.

The more you read that poem, the more it hurts. The solution
to such terrible things can also be found in story. Leonardo da
Vinci wrote a fable called *The Stone and the Steel* (1973) in which
he says: 'At last, very suddenly, there flashed forth a spark
which lit a marvellous fire, with the power to do marvellous
things.'

References

BARTHES, R. (1975) *S/Z* (London: Jonathan Cape).

BARZUN, J. (1971) *On Writing, Editing and Publishing: Essays Explicative and Hortatory* (Chicago University Press).
BETTELHEIM, B. (1976) *The Uses of Enchantment* (London: Thames & Hudson).
BRITTON, J. (1970) *Language and Learning* (London: Allen Lane).
BUBER, M. (1971) *I and Thou* (Edinburgh: T & T Clark).
CARLE, E. (1974) *The Very Hungry Caterpillar* (London: Puffin).
CAUSLEY, C. (1975) *Collected Poems* (London: Macmillan).
CHUKOVSKY, K. (1915) *From Two to Five* (California University Press, 1963).
DA VINCI, L. (1973) *Fables* (B. Nardini, ed.) (London: Collins).
DICKENS, C. (1854) *Hard Times* (London: Penguin, 1969).
DOCKAR-DRYSDALE, B. (1968) *Therapy in Child Care* (London: Longman).
FRYE, N. (1957) *Anatomy of Criticism* (Princeton University Press).
GARNER, A. (1965) *Elidor* (London: Collins, Armada Lion).
GARNER, A. (1977) *Tom Fobble's Day* (London: Collins).
GARNER, A. (1976) *The Stone Book* (London: Collins).
GREGORY, R. (1974) *Psychology: towards a Science of Fiction* in Margaret Meek, Aidan Warlow, Griselda Barton (eds) *The Cool Web* (London: The Bodley Head).
HARDY, B. (1975) *Tellers and Listeners* (London: Athlone Press).
HAUGAARD, E. C. (1974) *Complete Fairy Tales and Stories of Hans Christian Andersen* (London: Gollancz).
HAZEN, B. (1971) *The Sorcerer's Apprentice* (London: Methuen).
HEIDE, F. P. (1975) *The Shrinking of Treehorn* (London: Puffin).
HMSO (1984) *English from 5 to 16* (London: HMSO).
HMSO (1985) *The Curriculum from 5 to 16* (London: HMSO).
HUEY, E. B. (1908) *The Psychology and Teaching of Reading* (Boston: MIT Press, 1968).
HUGHES, S. (1977) *Dogger* (London: Puffin).
HUGHES. T. (1970) 'Myth and Education' in *Children's Literature in Education No. 1* (London: Ward Lock).
HUTCHINS, P. (1968) *Rosie's Walk* (London: The Bodley Head, Puffin).
JACKSON, D. (1978) *Ways of Talking* (London: Ward Lock).
LE GUIN, U (1971) *A Wizard of Earthsea* (London: Gollancz, Puffin).
MABEY, R. (1976) *Street Flowers* (London: Kestrel).
O'BRIEN, R. (1976) *Z for Zachariah* (London: Collins, Armada Lion).
PEARCE, P. (1970) *A Dog so Small* (London: Puffin).
PEARCE, P. (1984) *The Way to Sattin Shore* (London: Puffin).
ROSEN, H. (1984) *Stories and Meanings* (London: National Association for the Teaching of English).
SMITH, F. (1975) *Comprehension and Learning* (New York: Holt, Rinehart & Winston).
SOUTHALL, I. (1968) *Let the Balloon Go* (London: Puffin).
SPENCER, M. (1984) 'Speaking of Shifters' in M. Meek, J. Miller (eds) *Changing English: Essays for Harold Rosen* (London: Heinemann).
TOLKIEN, J. R. R. (1964) *Tree and Leaf* (London: Allen & Unwin).
VYGOTSKY, L. (1934) *Thought and Language* (Boston: MIT Press, 1962).
WINNICOTT, D. (1971) *Playing and Reality* (London: Tavistock).
ZOLOTOW, C. (1974) *My Grandson Lew* (London: World's Work).

Chapter 3

Something to Read About: The Content of Reading Schemes for Children

Sheila McCullagh

This paper accepts a definition of reading as 'making sense of written language'. It discusses themes and characters in stories for young children, and stresses the value of folk-tales, fairy tales and animal stories, as well as stories with child characters. It suggests that children's 'readers' or 'primers' should reflect such books as closely as possible, and indicates the way in which this may be done through a context-support approach to the teaching of reading.

In *The Use of Poetry and the Use of Criticism*, T. S. Eliot (1933) has this to say about writing: '. . . before you write you must have something to write about; which is a manifest truth frequently ignored by some of those who are trying to learn to write and by some of those who endeavour to teach writing.' It is surely also a manifest truth that in order to learn to read you must have something to read about. As Frank Smith says, 'there is one general answer to the question of how children learn to read, and that is *by making sense of written language*. A corollary to this statement is that children do not learn to read from nonsense.'

It is, therefore, of vital importance to consider what, in fact, we give young children to 'read about', in the first books we give them to read for themselves: the 'readers' (or 'primers') that they meet in school or at home, and with which we expect them to learn, for first experiences go deep and are often lasting in their effects.

How, then, are we teaching children to read? And what are we teaching them about books, through their early experiences?

Is the content of 'readers' such that they will learn to read, in the fullest meaning of that word, expecting the written symbols on the page to be as full of meaning for them as any spoken language? The problem is that their first books should not only be interesting; they must also be simple. They need to be what W. Hildick (1970) calls 'skill-acquiring instruments'. It is no use giving children the most fascinating book in the world, if it is too difficult for them to read. They will only do what we all do when faced with a task that seems impossibly difficult: having tried and failed, they will give up, decide that reading is not for them, and turn to some other activity.

but can be read together.

We have, therefore, to find some means to make it possible for children to find meaning in written language, to discover the rewards of reading, and at the same time so to arrange matters that the beginnings of reading for a child are not a series of steps, but a slope. → *upwards*

First, content. What are the 'rewards' of being able to read? What do we, as skilled readers, gain from reading? I suggest that we read for four main purposes: we read to find out facts; we read to widen our experience, both of the world and of other people; we read to discover more about ourselves; and we read for recreation and refreshment, in order, as it were, to take a holiday from our immediate surroundings.

The advantages of being able to read in order to find out factual information are clear to us all, living as we do in a world full of print, but for most of us, this is only a part of our reading. Narrative of one kind or another is important too. Even factual information can sometimes best be conveyed in the form of a story. Children have been known to teach themselves how to sail by reading Arthur Ransome. When information comes in the form of a story, it remains in the memory. I was talking to a vicar recently who told me that a bishop had once said to him, 'When you give a sermon, you can repeat it again in a year's time, because everyone will have forgotten what you said. But if you have included a story in that sermon, then you mustn't repeat it for seven years because everyone will remember the story.'

But there are more important things to be learnt from stories than factual information. As Hildick (1970) says, '. . . one good story is worth hundreds of non-fictional topic books, no matter how tastefully illustrated or attractively laid out, because for every Spanish galleon or Chippendale commode or lapwing's egg a child will be required to recognise in life there will be hundreds of Steerforths or Uriah Heeps or Huck Finns he will need to understand.' The attractions of a story are very strong for adults and particularly strong for children. As the Bullock Report (1975) declared, 'It was clear that the narrative mode provided for children of all ages the strongest motivation towards the reading of books.'

It is in the deepening of understanding of other people and of ourselves that reading is unique. It is only in reading that we find ourselves projected fully 'inside' another human being, looking out on the world through their eyes. Plays and television dramas show us other people from the outside. This is how we see them in our everyday lives. But in books we are taken inside the skin of other human beings. Their inmost thoughts and feelings are explicitly described, and so our experience is extended, and we develop an awareness of the feelings and reactions of others: a boy can discover what it is like to be a girl, and girls can find out through imaginative experience what it is like to be a boy. We can all experience life in other countries and in other times, or what it is like to belong to another race, if we can read stories written by the people who lived in those times and in those countries. It is no longer true to say that we only have one life to live; if we can read, we can, in imagination, lead many lives. Even though children's 'readers', and especially their early readers, are inevitably very simple, it is the skills which will lead to this kind of reading which they should foster. It is surely a mistake to say that children's 'readers' must only be about children who look like themselves, living in an environment which reflects their own with photographic precision. A child's imagination is capable of far more than this.

In the course of reading about others, we learn about ourselves. We discover that other people have the same thoughts and feelings as we do. Our sense of isolation is broken down, for when the feelings of characters in the story are made explicit, we often reognise them as our own. We are, through them, linked with other people.

Loneliness is more of a problem for human beings than is

often recognised, and this is surely true for many children. Much of the time they may be one of a gang, part of a group, part of a family, but at times many children feel isolated and lonely. Some young children cling to a special toy as a constant companion (and not only at night), while some even invent imaginary companions who are always with them. The characters in stories can be companions, too. They are always there, waiting for us. They are predictable, they never change. Perhaps that is one reason why children demand the same story over and over again, and read and re-read favourite books so often.

Through some stories, too, we may gain rest and refreshment. We are able to step, for a time, outside our immediate environment with all its problems, into the imaginary world of the story. This may sometimes be labelled 'escapism', but what of that? When we return to our own world we may be better able to enjoy it or endure it, or even to change it. There is nothing wrong with escaping. As J. R. R. Tolkien says, whether escape is good or bad depends on what you are escaping *from* and what you are escaping *to*.

If this is our experience of reading, then it follows that this is what we should be looking for in the stories we give our children, so that they may learn what 'reading' means. The books we read *to* children often contain opportunities for them to gain this kind of experience, and these should guide us in deciding what their first 'readers' should be about. For the books they first read for themselves should surely bear some relationship – even if only a slight one, but one as close as we can make it – to the kind of reading which will be possible for them later on. They should point in the right direction, and having – by reading *to* children – shown them the path that lies ahead, we should help children to cultivate the skills which will enable them to follow that path.

Stories in children's readers are sometimes divided into two categories: realistic stories and fantasy. This is surely a mistaken dichotomy; stories which appear on the surface to match the everyday world in which children live can be more remote from it than any fairy tale, and fantasy can contain truths about the 'real' world which every child can recognise. It is a long time since Nora Goddard (1958) confidently wrote:

'. . . the first books of a reading series should tell the story of the ordinary life of children in an ordinary family . . . This is familiar, secure ground and its appeal will be general.' We can no longer describe an 'ordinary family'. Perhaps we never could, and perhaps the children who read such books were never as interested in them as people assumed. As long ago as the eighteenth century, Dr Johnson, speaking of the moral fables written for the young, declared: 'Babies do not like to hear stories of babies like themselves, they require to have their imaginations raised by tales of giants and fairies and castles of enchantment.' The great Doctor may well have been right. Certainly it is the giants and castles of enchantment which have lasted down the years, rather than the moral fables. And today, many of the stories of 'ordinary children' are as much in realms of fantasy as is 'Jack and the Beanstalk' – in fact, Jack may be a good deal closer to children, in his adventuring out into a wider world, even if that world is a fantastic one.

Children do enjoy child characters in stories about families, and many such stories depict recognisably real children in real situations. If they are concerned with the fundamental feelings and experiences of childhood, they have a universal appeal. But the characters in the stories need not be limited to children, for children also identify with other creatures who are in the child's situation. For example, *The Story of Peter Rabbit* by Beatrix Potter, is attractive to young children not because it is about a young rabbit who goes into a garden, and is chased out by the gardener, though the action is swift and exciting; the story's appeal is surely because Peter Rabbit ventures out from home into a wider world, and breaks a prohibition – his mother has told him not to go into the garden. He escapes to safety (we no longer face our children with death, as the Victorians did), but he has to face the consequences: he loses his beautiful blue coat. This is a theme children can readily understand, for they, too, break prohibitions, and must at some time go from home into the world outside.

Children of any race and any country are on an equal footing in reading animal stories. They are even more so, when we give them folk-tales and fairy tales. It is not only that there are versions of the same fairy tale to be found in many parts of the world. We didn't have to worry about making sure that children's books contained people of other races, in the days when we gave them fairy tales to read. Such characters were the heroes and heroines of many stories. The fundamental appeal of such stories is their themes – the fact that they tell us about human beings and how they behave. And they do not show us only the good: greed and aggression and sheer folly are depicted too, and they are depicted in a way a young child can easily recognise; the characters are uncomplicated. The good are good, and the bad are bad, and what is more, the good always triumph and the bad are defeated, so that children, in identifying with the character who eventually comes out on top, find themselves identifying with the good. It is only as we grow older that we come to understand life is very much more complicated than this.

The settings may be fantastic, but this has advantages; they are not tied down to a particular time and place, and so they are *generalised*, and are equally relevant to children from different backgrounds and races; they form a common heritage, which we can all share, because the characters live in what are clearly imaginary worlds, which we can all enter. When they do enter them, children find recognition of their own thoughts and feelings. The stories have lasted because they are concerned with the human predicament. Their *themes* are true to human experience, even if their settings are fantastic.

In the *Uses of Enchantment*, Bruno Bettelheim (1976) made out a strong case for traditional folk and fairy tales, as stories which are close to the truth of children's feelings and children's lives. He points out that many young children have '. . . formless nameless anxieties and chaotic, angry and even violent fantasies . . . children know that they are not always good, and often when they are, they would prefer not to be.' So they may well find it easier to relate to the story of Cinderella than to the story of two perfectly-behaved children who never do anything wrong, because they know, from their own experience, all about jealousy.

There are many other situations in fairy stories which they recognise. When children first go to school, they leave the close circle of home and venture into a wider world. In many fairy tales, the hero is the third son, the ugly duckling, the neglected daughter who also has to get out into the world and who, with effort, overcomes difficulties and achieves happiness.

It is this richness and variety of stories which we should try to bring into the first books we give children to read for themselves. Not only will this provide the incentive for them to make the effort, to bring all their powers of learning and experience to bear in order to learn this new skill of reading, but it will also make it *possible* for them to learn, for reading is the extraction of meaning from written symbols, 'making sense of written language'.

How can this be done, when the first readers must also be 'skill-acquiring instruments'? First, a number of pressure groups have to be resisted. Many adults, recognising the importance of early experiences, demand that their special concerns should be included in the books children use in school. Many of these concerns are excellent in themselves. The danger is that they will impose a rigid structure on a story or series of stories, and so drain them of all life and interest for a child. Jane Austen once made up a mock plan for a novel, containing all the ingredients which people had, at one time or another, asked her to include. It was, of course, a nonsense. I have sometimes thought that I should make up a plan for a reading scheme on a similar basis. It would include many things.

There are the people who think that children and adults in a story should always behave perfectly, in order to set an appropriate pattern of behaviour for the children reading it. Such a story would probably be a very boring, and it would certainly be unrealistic – a point made in a letter to the *Guardian* by a parent who wrote: 'If only Janet would *hit* John!' Children need to learn how to conduct themselves, but they are surely more likely to learn from seeing the effects of wrong or foolish behaviour than they are by reading about paragons of virtue.

Then there are the people who demand that there shall be as many girls as boys in a story, and that the girls shall always be depicted as enterprising and triumphant. I have a certain sympathy with this point of view, because in our recent concentration on stories of 'ordinary families', the girls have generally been given rather a dull and subservient role, and one

modern schemes

that needs to be corrected. Such stories were never true to life. In the days when children were given fairy tales, there was no problem, as Little Red Riding Hood, Snow White, the Little Mermaid, Elisa (the sister of the brothers turned into wild swans) and many more bear witness. Like Kipling's sailor, they were people 'of infinite resource and sagacity'. And when to this demand is added a further one, that a story should include a girl and boy of every race, the chance of the text being a *real* story is small.

Again, I have sympathy with this point of view. Of course we need stories about people of other races and countries other than our own – if possible, stories written or told by people from those countries, rooted in their own experience; though, just as children can identify with children and creatures unlike themselves, so writers can imagine themselves inside people who are superficially unlike themselves, for we are all human beings, and we have our humanity in common. If that were not possible, women could only write about women, and men about men, and stories would be remarkably lop-sided. The more human experience the writer can bring to the creation of a character, even a character in a child's first 'reader', the better, but however determined the writer may be to promote good causes, all these things cannot be included in any *one* story. Stories should not be judged by the characters they *omit*. We should make good any omissions by choosing a variety of different stories for children to read.

There are two other important points to be borne in mind: first, if a story is to be one which sparks a child's imagination, it must first be forged in the imagination of the writer, and to do that, the writer has to call on his or her own experience. Secondly, for the story to be successful with children, it has to be written with an appreciation of a child's viewpoint: it has to look at the world through a child's eyes, even if the main characters are not children. Writers of such stories need not only to know children, but also to have a 'hot line' back into their own childhood, so that they remember vividly what it was like to be a child.

The second point is an important one. Let me give you an example of what I mean. In Margaret Donaldson's book, *Children's Minds* (1978), there is a quotation from Laurie Lee's

Cider with Rosie (1965), describing a child's experiences on his first day at school.

> I spent the first day picking holes in paper, then went home in a smouldering temper.
> 'What's the matter, Love? Didn't he like it at school, then?'
> 'They never gave me the present.'
> 'Present? What present?'
> 'They said they'd give me a present.'
> 'Well now, I'm sure they didn't.'
> 'They did! They said: "You're Laurie Lee, aren't you? Well just sit there for the present." I sat there all day but I never got it. I ain't going back there again.'

Here you have a piece of genuine childhood experience, truthfully remembered. You find a child who has not the necessary background experience to understand what the teacher said. And, as Margaret Donaldson points out, it is 'clear on very little reflection that the adult has also failed, at a deeper level, in understanding the child – in placing himself imaginatively at the child's point of view'. It is not easy, as an adult, to see through the eyes of a child, but it is important that the stories we choose for our children should have that perception.

There is another important point in Laurie Lee's description, which illuminates yet another problem in providing books, and especially the first books, for children learning to read. It shows how important *context* is, in understanding words. For many words can only be understood in context, and it is this which gives them meaning.

In learning to speak, children learn new words as part of a whole situation. 'Dog' is the creature running about, that they see and know. Children may not have the experience to know the meaning of a single word or phrase out of context, and even if they know one meaning, there may be others of which they are unaware, like Laurie Lee, or the eight-year-old girl, a good reader, who looked up from her book to say in an accusing tone: 'There's a mistake in this book. It says they *drank* the toast!' Words need to be presented in a context children find intelligible.

Context is linked to the whole problem of the form which early reading books should take, if they are to contain 'real stories' and at the same time be sufficiently simple for children to read. The only way in which this is possible, it seems to me, is to present the text which the child is going to read as part of a greater whole. If the words convey information, then they should be met in a situation in which children need that information – need it immediately, and for their own purposes. If the text tells a story, then it should be a part of a much fuller story, told largely through illustrations or through a longer version of the story read *to* the child.

Illustrations help children to build up, in their own minds, the imaginary world of the story – what Tolkien calls the 'secondary world', as distinct from the 'primary' world in which the children live. This is one of the skills of reading: we need to construct a new world inside our heads, and being able to do so is as important for the creative scientist as it is for the reader of fiction. Albert Einstein himself said, 'The gift of fantasy has meant more to me than my talent for absorbing positive knowledge.'

A child already has the ability to create an imaginary world through play. Someone for whom a tree-trunk or a chair becomes at will a flying horse, is not likely to find it difficult to imagine the secondary world of a story. He or she has only to learn to build it through words rather than things, through reading rather than through play.

Illustrations in the first 'readers' are of special importance, because they must convey character as well as the background setting. They often show much of the action, too, and they should be designed to give the child as many contextual clues as possible to the few words or phrases or sentences which accompany them. The whole story may also be read *to* the children by an adult, in a much fuller version than the one they are asked to read for themselves. In such a context, even the most banal sentence can take on a new and vivid meaning. For example, suppose you had read the children the story of Puss-in-Boots. Now suppose that you continued that story, to describe how Puss met a magician who had a flying carpet, a marvellous magic mat, and that anyone had only to step on it to be carried away to strange lands and adventures. Against the background of that story, even the simple sentence 'The cat sat on the mat' would take on a new meaning.

Set in the context of illustration and story, the possible themes and settings of children's first 'readers' are as many and various as those of any books for young children. They may not be 'great literature', but they can be as interesting as many of the stories that are read to children. Those based on the patterns of folk-tales and fairy tales will have another advantage, too. Folk-tales and fairy tales are full of rhymes and repetitions. The same thing is often done three times, or by three people, with very little variation, except perhaps for some change on the third occasion. Repetition of the same words is part of the story. It is unforced, and simply adds to the rhythm of the whole. Such stories are often written in a kind of rhythmic prose, which carries them along, and contains alliterative names and phrases, rhymes and songs which not only show the children that words which sound the same are often written with the same groups of letters, but which also remain in their memories, so that when they meet them again, they know what the printed words must be, even if they cannot immediately recognise them in the text. And so their confidence is built up, as well as their reading vocabulary.

In talking about writing for children, Gillian Avery (1971) told the story of a distinguished general who was asked to name the children's book that had meant most to him: 'He said that he had long ago lost sight of the one he had really treasured, and all he could remember of it now was the couplet

'Pingo sat in the wood of Pottle
With strawberry juice in a thermos bottle.'

Which shows not only the power of rhyme to linger in the memory, but also that children's stories don't necessarily have to be great literature to be enjoyed and treasured.

Humour is another ingredient which makes a story attractive. A book which is really funny can lift our spirits, and it can do the same for children. They enjoy the downfall of the great and the pompous even more than we do, and this is the very stuff of many fairy tales.

So, even in the very early readers, children can be given things to enjoy, and they can be made aware of the rhythms of sentences. These rhythms will help them to read in meaningful phrases, while rhymes will draw their attention to the similarities and differences between words. The action of the story should be swift, so that something happens on every page, and the *themes* of the stories, though not necessarily always their setting, should be rooted in the experiences of childhood. In this way, we shall give our children something to read *about*, and in doing so, make reading itself possible.

References

AVERY, G. (1971) 'Writing for children: a social engagement?' *Children's literature in education* (Agathom Press Inc., New York), p. 20.

BETTELHEIM, B. (1976) *The Uses of Enchantment* (London: Thames and Hudson), p. 7.

BULLOCK REPORT (1975) *A Language for Life* (London: HMSO).

DONALDSON, M. (1978) *Children's Minds* (Glasgow: Collins, Fontana Books), p. 17.

ELIOT, T. S. (1933) *The Use of Poetry and the Use of Criticism* (London: Faber and Faber), p. 55.

GODDARD, N. (1958) *Reading in the Modern Infant School* (Oxford University Press).

HILDICK, W. (1970) *Children and Fiction* (London: Evans Bros.), p. 8.

LEE, L. (1965) *Cider with Rosie* (London: The Hogarth Press), p. 50.

SMITH, F. (1978) *Reading* (Cambridge University Press).

TOLKIEN, J. R. R. (1947) *Essays Presented to Charles Williams* (Oxford University Press).

Chapter 4

Spot and Pat: Living in the Best Company When You Read

Cliff Moon

Discussion about the relative merits of reading schemes and what are commonly referred to as 'real books', as resources for early reading instruction, has heightened in recent years. This paper outlines the background to the debate, raises some key issues underlying it and suggests that three kinds of consideration are emerging from related research and commentary: syntactic, semantic and affective. Finally, a children's picture book by the author/illustrator Pat Hutchins, is presented as a satisfactory embodiment of all three considerations.

> **Live always in the best company when you read.**
> Reverend Sydney Smith (1771–1845)

We live in paradoxical times. Five new reading schemes will be published by leading UK educational publishers in the coming months. *The Times Educational Supplement* has just published a series of articles on 'excellent' primary schools. On 17 May 1985, Chamberlayne Wood School, Brent was described thus:

> English is about reading and a great deal of writing and talking – *but there are no reading schemes* and no comprehension exercises.

Whilst at Northborough Primary in Cambridgeshire (24 May 1985):

> The approach to reading changed radically last year. *All reading schemes and colour coding were abandoned.* Instead, books were grouped into three categories – for lower, middle and upper schools. Each category had a wide range

of difficulty, and children were to be allowed to choose any book they wanted.

And writing about their classroom organisation of reading resources two practising primary teachers recently had these things to say about 'real books' – neither have used reading schemes for some years:

> ### INFANTS
> I used to colour code the published books belonging to our school according to approximate readability levels . . . Now we no longer try to grade books, other than by housing most of our very simple picture books together in one reading area . . . non-fiction in a second reading area and schools' library service books in a third. All the rest are together in the largest reading area.
>
> (Ashworth, 1985, p. 13)
>
> ### JUNIORS
> I don't grade books. Books are to do with the meanings that are in the heads of the children who read them and I can't grade those.
>
> (Baker, 1985, p. 17)

So on the one hand the publication of graded reading schemes is still a growth industry, whilst on the other we find an increasing number of teachers successfully planning their children's reading development, not only without schemes, but without recourse to readability grading either. The rationale which underpins their teaching has both a distinguished history and theoretical base.

Background

At the turn of the century, a psychologist was calling for the disappearance of reading schemes, largely on the grounds that 'no trouble has been taken to write that what the child would naturally say about the subject in hand, nor indeed, to say anything connectedly or continuously' (Huey, 1908). In 1970 a book was published which demolished every major scheme in use at the time (Thomson, 1970) and the Bullock Report (1975) subsequently made this statement about reading schemes:

> We are certainly not advocating that the school should necessarily use one, and we welcome the enterprise of those schools which have successfully planned the teaching of reading without the use of a graded series. (7.25)

A seminal work by Spencer (1976), alias Meek, analysed the two-fold mismatch between the reading scheme books which are provided as children enter formal schooling and the stories they have had, or are having, read to them by adults, as well as the verbal stories they have composed for themselves from a very early age. It is worth quoting one of her conclusions, bearing in mind that it was published almost ten years ago:

> The crucial difference between the present situation and any that has gone before is illustrated by the extraordinary pressure exerted upon children to become literate, and the incredible wealth of books for young children which exemplify, not the generality of pre-school experience, but the individuality and endless vitality of storytelling. Yet the service of the latter is so little called on to advance the cause of the former. Our most pressing unsolved problem is to define and exemplify the place of children's literature in literacy. (p. 21)

We have seen a number of attempts to solve that problem in recent years and notable among them is the work of Bennett (1979, 1980). Donaldson (1978, p. 115) assured us that there was a 'substantial amount of evidence' supporting the view that an activity should be intrinsically rewarding for it to be sustained and enjoyed in the future. Extrinsic rewards might lead to success in the present but rejection later. This has clear implications for the content of what beginners are expected to read. It can no longer be argued that content is unimportant so long as skills are learnt – that the rewards will come later. It has frequently been claimed that many children have been put off reading during the process of learning to read. Why else would a Schools Council (Southgate *et al.*, 1981) and two Assessment of Performance Unit Reports (1981, 1982) lead HMI (1982, p. 9) to conclude that the teaching of literature should now receive greater attention in primary schools?

Indeed it was this very observation that children were learning to dislike reading as they acquired competence which led to the organic development of an individualised approach to reading at Hillfields Primary School, Bristol where I taught in the early 1970s and which later resulted in the publication of comparative lists of selected books for young readers (Moon, 1973–85). Meek (1982) sums this up most aptly when she claims:

> What the beginner reader reads makes all the difference to his view of reading. (p. 11)

and:

> The way children are taught to read tells them what adults think literacy is. (p. 18)

Books and learning to read

So what do we think literacy is and in the light of that, which book resources are most likely to help, rather than hinder, children's literacy development? Instead of attempting a comprehensive review of our current understanding of the literacy-learning process (see Moon in prep.) I should like to set up some fictitious examples of what commonly occurs in *contemporary* reading schemes and pose questions about underlying assumptions. By inventing examples no offence will be given to well-meaning authors and publishers, but what I and others believe to be crucial issues will be raised.

Example 1

Having studied the work of Clay (1972), a publisher decides to incorporate into a reading scheme a book which will teach children how stories work and how books are read from front to back and top to bottom (only in Eurocentric cultures, of course).

Here is the result:

Page 1 This is a book
Page 2 It tells a story

Page 3 Look at its left page
Page 4 Look at its right page
Page 5 The end

Remember that although this example is fictitious, it is based on an actual publication which is less than ten years old.

Question 1

Is this what children need to know in order to cope with the structures of stories and books? Would not the wordless picture books of artists like Raymond Briggs and Brian Wildsmith do the job infinitely better?

Example 2

Deciding that early readers should incorporate a 'controlled vocabulary' in order to build up children's 'sight vocabulary' a publisher devises a hide-and-seek type of book which asks questions of the pictures:
Is he there?
No, not there.
Is he there?
No, not there.
Is he there?
No, not there.

Question 2

What kind of learning theory underpins concepts of 'controlled vocabulary' and 'sight vocabulary'? Would not Eric Hill's *Where's Spot?* (1980) be less difficult to read and more likely to develop competence and confidence? The book has a similar format but asks questions like:
Is he inside the clock?
Is he under the bed?
Is he in the box?
Are words like *clock*, *bed* and *box* more difficult than *there* when the objects are clearly illustrated on each page? Isn't this text closer to what the child would naturally say (Huey, 1908)?

Example 3

Heeding what Southgate *et al.* (1981) and the APU Reports
(1981, 1982) found about the formation of negative attitudes
towards reading in the primary years, a publisher seeks to
sermonise at the end of each book and indoctrinate children
with the notion that reading is fun, that they must enjoy it and
repeat it. On the last page we have:
  'I like this play,' said the Queen of Hearts.
  'I'll read it again and learn all the parts.'
Whether or not the book bears re-reading is never considered –
the message is simply 'get on and do it'.

Question 3

Can children learn to love reading (or anything) merely
because they are told they have to? Should not the intrinsic
merits of books themselves lead children to want to re-read
them? Why do children re-read time and again Maurice
Sendak's *Where the Wild Things Are?* or David McKee's *Not Now,
Bernard?*

It is not my intention to attempt answers to the questions posed
by these three examples but rather to outline some recent
observations by researchers and commentators which may
help us to understand them better. For convenience I have
grouped these under three headings: syntactic, semantic and
affective considerations.

Syntactic considerations

Current research is beginning to shed light on the knowledge
about print which young children bring to the reading task.
Ferreiro and Teberosky (1983) and Ferreiro (1984) report a
variety of Piagetian-style investigations carried out in
Switzerland, Argentina and Mexico and their findings are
supported by similar work in France, Israel, Canada, Spain
and the United States (Goodman, 1985). Briefly, they are
discovering that well before formal schooling commences,

children have formed concepts about how print works and what it is used for. At an early age they hypothesise, for example, that a word must have three or more letters for it to be 'readable', that 'readable' text must consist of *different* letters and that the length of a word must relate to the size of the object to which it refers. I have reported elsewhere (Moon, 1985, p. 6) what happened when children in a Reading, Berkshire nursery class were presented with a book which depicted individual animals with a single-word caption beneath each:

Page 1   Elephant
Page 2   Lion
Page 3   Tiger
Page 4   Crocodile
Page 5   Giraffe, etc.

Transcripts of the children 'reading' this book revealed that they did one of two things. They either narrated a story based on the picture sequence:

'Once upon a time there was an elephant who lived in a forest. One day the elephant went out and met a lion. He said, 'Hello, lion, shall we go for a walk?'
'Yes,' said the lion, so they walked along the path until they came to a tiger' . . . etc.

Or they said:

'This is an elephant'
'This is a lion'
'This is a tiger'
'This is a crocodile'
'This is a giraffe', etc.

An alternative version began '*Here* is an elephant', etc. It is interesting to note that none of these three- and four-year-olds read the text as it was printed and it could be argued that their expectations of the book were more sophisticated than those the author had of his/her readers.

Another example of the syntactic expectations which novice readers bring to text is illustrated by a tape I heard of a child attempting to read:

The dog plays with the ball.
I like to play with the dog.

This child adamantly refused to read *dog* at the end of the second line despite his teacher's constant exhortation, 'But, you've just read that word here – look at it – it's the *same* word as this . . .' and so on. She kept pointing to *dog* at the beginning of the first sentence but the boy would (could?) not accept that it was the same word. Why? I think there are a number of things happening here and I shall briefly mention just three of them:

1. The child was processing the *meaning* of the sentences, not the *words* as visual entities. The word *dog* has a different function and position in both sentences therefore how could it be 'the same'?

2. A prior expectation of a certain syntactic pattern had been built up where *ball* was the most obvious alternative but the boy had sufficient knowledge of phoneme/grapheme relationships to realise that the word was not *ball*. Crystal (1976) has referred to this as a 'syntactic complexity variable of preceeding linguistic context'.

3. The teacher is assuming that novice readers read the *words*, unlike fluent readers who attend to other things – try reading today's newspaper aloud if that seems unacceptable! Remember Meek's (1982) claim that the 'first thing is not to get the words right but to get the story right'. Isn't that what this child is trying to do? Why can't his teacher recognise that?

Semantic considerations

When Stebbing and Raban (1982) analysed children's oral reading miscues and recall rates after reading comparable stories from two reading schemes – *Through the Rainbow* (1966) and *One Two Three and Away* (1963) – they found statistical differences in qualitative miscues and recall, both favouring the *One Two Three and Away* story. In discussing their results the authors say this of the *Through the Rainbow* text:

> Although the text has a fictional surface, it is in fact a narrative without structure. There is no plot requiring

resolution . . . There is no introductory 'Once upon a
time . . .' or anything suggestive of development . . . The
characters are insubstantial and little occurs in the train of
events to make the reader wonder what will happen next.
(p. 159)

It is interesting to note that they compared two reading scheme
stories. Similar comparisons between scheme stories and 'real
books' might well show more marked contrasts.

Applebee (1980) examined the verbal narratives of two- to
five-year-olds and concluded that:

By the time they come to school, children ordinarily have a
firmly developed set of expectations about what a story *is*.

This is not restricted to expectations about the conventions of
written stories, which will obviously be better developed in
children who have been regularly read to. *All* children
constantly invent stories in their pre-school years, as we well
know from the Bristol Language Development Project (Wells,
1981) data. Incidentally, another universal which has recently
come to light is that all children on entry to formal schooling are
much   more   proficient   at   handling   environmental   print
(cartons, signs, TV adverts, etc.) than they are at handling
print in books (Goodman and Altwerger, 1981; Haussler, 1984)
and this has prompted Goodman (1985) to suggest that one
way to abandon the tradition of literacy for an élite is to
recognise what all children know, and work from that
knowledge base rather than one which is culturally and
domestically specific to certain childrn. All this leads to the
fascinating speculation that the reading scheme of the future
should be based on empty cartons, weekly trips to the
supermarket and the transcription of children's own stories!

Wade (1982) compared a typical reading scheme text with a
John Burningham picture/story book. He discovered that the
scheme story could be printed equally well back-to-front and
inside-out whereas the Burningham text, short as it was, could
only work in a forward-moving manner. The author remarks
on:

the potential conflict in the minds of children caused by
any reading which promotes arbitrariness instead of

pattern, disconnection rather than coherence and emptiness rather than fulfilment. (pp. 33–4)

Those three words, *pattern, coherence* and *fulfilment* might serve as useful criteria when selecting reading resources for beginner readers. Wade concludes:

> I would criticise materials of the 'See Spot. Run Spot. Run' variety not only because, as Halliday (1969) says, they bear little relation to the language as a child has learned to use it. Additionally they make of narrative something apart from life as it is lived and they turn the food of story into a dry biscuit. (p. 36)

Affective considerations

Moss (1977) describes how her adopted daughter became deeply attached to a dubiously-written tale about a kitten called Peppermint. As it turned out, Alison loved the story because it mirrored her own life experience and she was able to empathise with Peppermint, thereby coming to understand herself, her fears and relationships in ways to which previously she had been denied access. Bruner (1984) points out that reading schemes seldom, if ever, contain material to which the child can respond emotionally, yet this is one experience which reading offers most powerfully. He asks:

> What, indeed, is *Run Jane run. Catch the ball.* about? (p. 199)

and concludes:

> My suggestion is that we begin by making reading an instrument for entering possible worlds of human experience – as drama, story, or tale – in order to bring it as close as possible to the forms in which children already know spoken language best. And just as the human condition is the favourite topic of human reflection, so the text depicting that condition can become the basis of that reflection. (p. 200)

In case you are thinking that is all very well in relation to an adult's reading of Doris Lessing or John Fowles I shall conclude by quoting the complete text of *Titch* by Pat Hutchins (1972), a children's picture book which, in my view, epitomises the syntactic, semantic and affective qualities which ought to be evident in *every* text we put before a novice reader.

Titch

Titch was little.
Her sister Mary was a bit bigger.
And his brother Pete was a lot bigger.
Pete had a great big bike.
Mary had a big bike.
And Titch had a little tricycle.
Pete had a kite that flew high above the trees.
Mary had a kite that flew high above the houses.
And Titch had a pinwheel that he held in his hand.
Pete had a big drum.
Mary had a trumpet.
And Titch had a little wooden whistle.
Pete had a big saw.
Mary had a big hammer.
And Titch held the nails.
Pete had a big spade.
Mary had a fat flowerpot.
But Titch had the tiny seed.
And Titch's seed grew
and grew
and grew.

References

APPLEBEE, A. N. (1980) 'Children's Narratives: New Directions' in *The Reading Teacher*, vol. 34, no. 2, November.

APU (1981 & 1982) *Language Performance in Schools: Primary Survey Reports Nos 1 & 2* (London: HMSO).

ASHWORTH, L. (1985) 'Teaching Infants to Read' in *Practical Ways to Teach: Reading* (C. Moon, ed.) ch. 1 (London: Ward Lock Educational).

BAKER, A. (1985) 'Developing Reading With Juniors' in *Practical Ways to Teach: Reading* (C. Moon, ed.) ch. 2 (London: Ward Lock Educational).

BENNETT, J. (1979 & 1980) *Learning to Read with Picture Books* and *Reaching Out*, 1st edn (London: Thimble Press).

BRUNER,J. (1984) 'Language, mind and reading' in H. Goelman, A. Oberg & F. Smith (eds) *Awakening to Literacy* (London: Heinemann), pp. 193–200.

BULLOCK REPORT (1975) *A Language for Life* (London: HMSO)

CLAY, M. M. (1972) *Reading: The Patterning of Complex Behaviour* (London: Heinemann).

CRYSTAL, D. (1976) *Child Language, Learning and Linguistics* (London: Edward Arnold).

DONALDSON, M. (1978) *Children's Minds* (London: Fontana).

FERREIRO, E. (1984) 'The underlying logic of literacy development' in H. Goelman, A. Oberg & F. Smith (eds) *Awakening to Literacy* (London: Heinemann), pp. 154–173.

FERREIRO, E. and TEBEROSKY, A. (1983) *Literacy Before Schooling* (Heinemann: London).

GOODMAN, K. S. (1985) 'Growing into literacy' in *Prospects 53*, vol. XV, no. 1 (UNESCO).

GOODMAN, Y. and ALTWERGER, B. (1981) *Print Awareness in Pre-School Children* Program in Language and Literacy, Occasional Paper 4 (University of Arizona).

HALLIDAY, M. A. K. (1969) 'Relevent models of language' in *Educational Review*, vol. 22, no. 1, pp. 26–37.

HAUSSLER, M. (1984) *Transitions into Literacy* Program in Language and Literacy, Occasional Paper 10 (University of Arizona).

HILL, E. (1980) *Where's Spot?* (London: Heinemann).

HMI (1982) *Bullock Revisited* (London: DES).

HUEY, E. B. (1908) *The Psychology and Pedagogy of Reading*, (1908). Reprinted 1968 by MIT Press.

HUTCHINS, P. (1972) *Titch* (London: The Bodley Head).

McKEE, D. (1980) *Not Now, Bernard* (London: Andersen Press).

MEEK, M. (1982) *Learning to Read* (London: The Bodley Head).

MOON, C. (1973–85) *Individual Reading* (Centre for the Teaching of Reading, University of Reading) (1st edn 1973; 17th edn 1985).

MOON, C. (ed.) (1985) *Practical Ways to Teach: Reading* (London: Ward Lock Educational).

MOON, C. (in preparation) 'The teaching of reading: where are we now?' in M. Meek & C. Mills, *Language and Literacy in the Primary School* (London: Falmer Press).

MOSS, E. (1977) 'What is a "good" book?' in M. Meek, A. Warlow & G. Barton, *The Cool Web: The Pattern of Children's Reading* (London: The Bodley Head), pp. 140–2.

SENDAK, M. (1967) *Where the Wild Things Are* (London: The Bodley Head/Picture Puffins).

SOUTHGATE, V., ARNOLD, H. and JOHNSON, S. (1981) *Extending Beginning Reading* (London: Heinemann for Schools Council).

SPENCER, M. (1976) 'Stories are for telling' in *English in Education*, vol. 10, no. 1, Spring, pp. 16–23.

STEBBING, J. and RABAN, B. (1982) 'Reading for meaning, an investigation of the effect of narrative in two reading books for seven year olds' in *Reading*, vol. 16, no. 3, pp. 153–161.

THOMSON, B. (1970) *Learning to Read* (London, Sidgwick & Jackson).

WADE, B.(1982) 'Reading rickets and the uses of story' in *English in Education*, vol. 16, no. 3, pp. 28–37.

WELLS, G. (1981) *Learning Through Interaction* (Cambridge University Press).

Part II

Implications for the Teachers of Reading

Chapter 5

Reading Research as a Resource for the Teacher

Elizabeth Goodacre

This paper describes in-service work with teachers which explored their expectations about the part of the course dealing with research. Information was gathered on their expectations about the content, teaching method and rationale for including research. Using a sentence-completion activity the teachers demonstrated a variety of attitudes to research, ranging from favourable to markedly unfavourable. Asked to suggest a number of resources for teaching and rank them in order of importance, research was not highly rated. The way in which the topic of reading research was treated on these courses is described, including 'feedback' from the teachers about the effectiveness of the format adopted. The paper concludes with a discussion of recent ideas regarding the difference between researchers' and teachers' knowledge and the role that expectations can play in teaching interactions, which are seen as basically reciprocal in nature.

Background

I have had the privilege for a number of years of being invited to contribute to the one-month in-service training courses held twice a year at the Centre for the Teaching of Reading (University of Reading). Usually I have been asked to contribute a session on 'reading research' to the course programme. Since 1968 I have produced an annual *Review of Reading Research* for the Centre. This publication is printed and sold by the Centre, and provides a summary and annotated list of the research published in book form and journals in Britain each year.

I have found talking to the teachers on these one-month courses a valuable experience, both for clarifying my own views on the function of research and for the opportunity to share teaching experiences and discuss educational issues, as course members have a variety of experience in teaching reading. However, I have found the task of giving a session on 'reading research' a daunting one, particularly as each year I have become more aware of the 'knowledge explosion' and the variety of sources of information about how children learn to read. Increasingly a primary aim for me has been to encourage in teachers an understanding of the nature and type of information that comes from research activities, and the differences and similarities with knowledge gained from classroom experience. In recent years, as part of such sessions I have tried to explore course members' attitudes to research and to use the knowledge gained in this way as a launching pad for the main content of the session – usually a discussion of research methodology and implications for teaching, illustrated by particular studies relevant to the group's interests and experience. In this paper, I should like to share with you some of the information I have collected about these teachers' attitudes to reading research, their expectations, and the extent to which they viewed research as a 'resource'. In the second part of the paper, I should like to consider some recent ideas about teachers and teaching and the extent to which attributing specific characteristics to reading research is likely to be related to the learner's educational experience.

Teachers' expectations about and attitudes towards reading research

Expectations

At the start of each session, members were asked to write down briefly for me their replies to the following questions:

(a) WHAT do you expect today's sessions will be about (content)?
(b) HOW do you think it will be done (teaching method/s)?
(c) WHY do you think this is on the programme (rationale)?

These expectations were then shared between course members in twos and fours and then in a large group discussion with me. At the end of the day, teachers individually agreed to hand in their written replies for me to read and analyse at a later date.

The following analysis is based on the sessions spent with the two most recent courses at the Centre (1985 groups).

(a) Content

81% mentioned the words 'latest', 'current', 'new', 'now' or 'up-to-date';

26% referred to 'an overview', 'summary' or 'survey';

15% wanted it to be relevant to their teaching;

 7% thought the content should include evaluation;

 7% had assumed the session would be about the tutor's own research.

(Some teachers mentioned more than one element in describing their expectations of the content.)

(b) Method

41% thought this would be by lecture/talk;

37% that group discussion in some form would be used;

26% by practical work of some sort/activities;

 7% use of handouts;

 7% use of OHPs.

(c) Rationale

44% so members could keep up-to-date;

15% to enable members to evaluate or modify their own practice;

 7% because teachers need some theory on which to base their practice;

(A number of the replies reiterated their answers to the content question, implying the rationale was self-evident.)

The general picture emerging was that these teachers expected that they were in need of updating in their knowledge, that about one in four hoped for some sort of review or summary from the 'expert', that this would be likely to be conveyed by conventional means of communicating straight information – the lecture – but that discussion and/or practical activities of some sort would break up the anticipated one-way form of communication.

Concepts of 'reading research'

One activity that course members were asked to carry out was a sentence completion 'test'. (This was used as a way into talking about reading tests and 'test anxiety' and other forms of reading achievement, such as reading attitudes and how to quantify them.) Members were asked to complete with one word answers the following:

Cooking is
Football is
Micros are
Reading is
Cricket is
Books are
Reading research is
Television is
I am

Analysing the teachers' responses, as might be expected 'books' and 'reading' received a 'good press'. For example, on Summer course N26, 1985 – sixteen different, positive words were used to describe 'books', two-thirds of the group using the words 'fascinating', 'fun', 'important', 'informative' and 'interesting'; for 'reading', twelve favourable words were used, half the group describing reading as 'enjoyable', 'interesting', or 'pleasurable', although one member did reply with the completion word 'slow'!

Percentage of Group	*Summer 1985* *N26*	*Spring 1985* *N23*	*Summer 1984* *N21*
Controversial/contradictory	4	4	10
Interesting/fascinating/ eye-opening/thought provoking	23	17	38
Good/useful/important/valuable	38	4	0
Necessary	11	4	0
Complicated/complex/involved	11	9	10
Long/extensive	4	0	5
Difficult/hard/confusing	0	35	10
Futile/boring/tedious/pretentious	0	17	5
Distant/far-off/impractical	4	9	19
Other	4	0	5

FIGURE 5.1   *Words teachers used to describe reading research*

Figure 5.1 shows the distribution of different words used to describe reading research for three different groups (1984–85). It can be seen that the groups differed in relation to the proportion of favourable/unfavourable words used. No explanation can be offered for these differences, other than that there may have been more members of the Summer 1985 group who had themselves been involved in research (diploma/higher degree studies). Some members of this group mentioned this, but such information was not available for the other two groups.

I found it difficult to decide how 'controversial/ contradictory' might be classified – whether it is indicative of a basically favourable or unfavourable attitude. However, I think the above figure does suggest that in each group, there was a sizeable proportion of teachers who had a schema or construct of reading research in terms of attributes of complexity and difficulty, and in two of the three groups, several teachers were prepared to categorise such research as 'futile, tedious, pretentious and boring'. (An example of the category 'other' was the teacher who responded 'Reading research is Monday' – the day of the week on which the session occurred!)

Reading research as a 'resource'

In one course group, a list of nine 'resources' for teaching was built up on the blackboard. The 'resources' in the order suggested by the teachers were:

1. Books/materials
2. Colleagues
3. Time
4. Teacher (qualities, etc.)
5. (Learning) environment
6. Parents
7. Community
8. Learner/s (abilities, etc.)
9. Media.

I asked them to add reading research to the list, and then to rank the 'resources' in order of importance. The result is shown in Figure 5.2.

		Mean
1.	Learner	1.79
2.	Teacher	2.71
3.	Books/Materials	2.93
4.	Time	4.07
5.	Parents	5.2
6.	Environment	6.29
7.	Colleagues	6.7
8.	Reading Research	8.29
9.	Media	8.36
10.	Community	8.64

FIGURE 5.2   *Teachers' ranking of resources for teaching*

Kyriacou (1985) in a paper entitled 'Conceptualising research on effective teaching' describes teaching in terms of process and outcome and the relevance of considering a framework of context. He reports on 'context variables' of a lesson influencing teacher and pupil behaviour. The variables suggested by his teachers are similar – teacher characteristics (experience, knowledge); pupil characteristics (age, ability); class (range of ability, size); subject (topic, difficulty level); school (ethos, size); community (urban, rural, affluence); occasion (weather, time of day).

The rankings I obtained might suggest that reading research is seen as something external to the classroom and even rated on average less highly than the pupil's parents. Research was seen as something fairly external to the normal teaching situation, although possibly a resource available for exploitation.

Feedback from the teachers

In two course groups, teachers were asked for written 'feedback' at the end of the day, about the effectiveness of the sessions provided.

Group A There were various comments about the unexpectedness of the format adopted (not conforming to 'straight lecture' expectations). A particular aspect of classroom practice, familiar to most of the teachers present ('hearing children read') had been chosen to illustrate changing methodology and models of reading used in research. Types of research were described, including ethnographic studies, and how data could be collected, including the use of tape transcripts. This concentration on research and a particular aspect of classroom practice drew a number of comments:

> 'Very thought provoking after initial confusion.'

> 'Not at all what I expected . . . very down to earth and understandable. Research will hopefully not be so off putting in the future.'

> 'It's been very valuable . . . I've enjoyed your presentation and feel I've benefited from this "look" at one aspect of reading research. Hope my children will benefit too.'

> 'I recognise myself in so much you have been talking about this afternoon. I half expected not to understand the lecture. I thoroughly enjoyed it.'

> 'I feel less afraid of research after listening to you talk about it, and realise now that we are all researchers in our own classrooms even if it is for our own benefit alone.'

> 'Research can be presented in such a way that many judgements can be drawn from it. Transcripts (raw material) seem more relevant . . . perhaps nearer the bone . . . to see ourselves as others see us.'

Comment was made on the function of the tutor's experience and approach:

> 'Far less academic than I expected . . . I could understand it and enjoyed it . . . it was easier to relate to someone who is a researcher who has actually worked in an infant classroom.'

> 'It does seem that one of the ways to stop education research being scary/distant from practitioners is to convey the excitement of the studies via enthusiasm such as your own.'

The expression of such feelings on the part of the tutor may of course, be related to the response obtained from the group, to their role in the interactive process going on in the 'lecture room'.

Some teachers thought selection of information was important, but there were various views about this:

> 'I do find, time to actually read and inwardly digest research material is my greatest problem, therefore annotations provide me with a way to decide which studies I will make the time for.'

> 'As a class teacher I have often been left feeling inadequate in some way, after reading research. I shall now choose carefully the research I read in relation to the age group and situation in which I teach . . . very valuable.'

Comments arose about the expectation that specific research rather than research in general would be dealt with:

> 'Thought it would be more specific to and about certain research, not about research in general. . . .'

> 'Expected more information on research that's been conducted rather than methods employed . . . having said that, it's interesting to be given an overview of methods/pitfalls/analysis/steps in research. I'm not sure I shall use it directly but my perspective, as with so much of this course, has been broadened and possibly altered.'

Group B   This group made similar points but in addition commented on the placing of the session:

> 'Useful in concentrating on approach to the nature of research as opposed to being bombarded with more research results . . . better in week one.'

> 'A useful summary of different models of research, it fits well with the point we have reached at this stage of the course.'

Implications of research – can you generalise?

> 'I feel that research is only valuable to a teacher when she can see any ideas are practicable.'

'I do not always understand the whys and wherefores of the research but I do want to know the practical implications . . . some I might reject but some I will accept. I am a class teacher and must admit I don't always understand the theory.'

'Made me realise how far I am from research . . . I'm constantly falling between two stools of thought because my mind repeatedly refers back to the children in school, their differences and similarities, their needs. I find I cannot move away from the practicalities of the classroom, needs of the children in difficulties, the teacher/child interaction . . . circumstances alter cases, making it difficult to be rigid in your approach.' (Possibly this teacher means consistency in approach? Certainly I think he/she is expressing something of the pragmatic nature of teacher knowledge compared with that of the researcher. The 'particularistic' nature of the teacher's perspective has been described by A. S. Bolster (1983) in a *Harvard Educational Review* article entitled 'Toward a more effective model of research on teaching'.)

Is information on reading research effective if at least it encourages reflection on practice?

It makes you think about what you do in the classroom, whether you really do what you think you do . . . its the ACTUAL THINKING ABOUT WHAT we do that I think was most important!' [Capitals were used by the writer.]

Changing conceptions of teaching, and communication and research knowledge

M. Lampert (1985) writes about the work of teaching and how society tends to believe in the existence of solutions for every problem. She argues that social science researchers and government policy-makers have turned away from conflicts that might arise in the classroom and assume that the teacher is

a technician–production manager who has the responsibility for
monitoring the efficiency with which learning is being
accomplished. In this view, teaching can be improved if
practitioners use researchers' knowledge to solve classroom
problems. The teacher's work is to find out what researchers
and policy-makers say should be done with or to students and
then do it. . . . If the teacher does what she is told, students will
learn. However, in practice, it is not as simple as that! Teachers
are concerned with the expectations, often conflicting, of
different groups – individual learners, their parents, the
Headteacher and colleagues, local and central government
requirements and legislation. As Lampert points out 'one needs
to have the resources to cope with equally weighted alternatives
when it is not appropriate to express a preference between
them. One needs to be able to take advice from researchers but
also know what to do when that advice is contradictory, or
when it contradicts knowledge that can only be gained in a
particular content . . . One needs to be comfortable with a self
that is complicated and sometimes inconsistent.'

Our knowledge, beliefs and expectations tend to determine
how we interpret new information and experiences. Generally,
people are likely to evade, distort or ignore extremely
discrepant information, discredit the source, or generate a
separate schema for the discrepant information. Indeed, R.
Anderson *et al.* (1977) concluded that 'from the perspective of
schema theory, the principle determinant of the knowledge a
person can acquire . . . is the knowledge he/she possesses'. This
could suggest that teachers who read research, do it, or have an
exploratory view of their own teaching ('we are all researchers in
our own classrooms') will be more 'open' to reading research
information and knowledge.

Learners' schemas also bias the weight, credibility and
validity they give to information. Schemas lead, for example, to
what Ross (1977) has described as the common 'basic
attribution error'. This is giving more weight to evidence which
helps explain behaviour in terms of disposition rather than
situation. P. H. Johnston (1985) discusses this in a recent paper
'Understanding reading disability'. He describes the 'trait/
state' notions in personality psychology and how for teachers it
may be more valuable to use behaviour explanations of the

'state' type, which imply characteristics which potentially can be changed by education, than 'trait' explanations in terms of the individual learners' rates of mental processing. He concentrates in his paper on the degree to which reading disability is likely to result from a combination of conceptual difficulties, rational and irrational use of self-defeating strategies and negative affective responses on the part of the learner.

G. Salomon (1981), in *Communication and Education – Social and Psychological Interactions*, discusses the way in which general schemas and what might be termed 'superordinate schemas', can be formed through instruction, and are not then easily modified. He suggests that it can be hypothesised that teaching which systematically emphasises the ONE right answer, the ONE correct way of learning, or the ONE proper way to evaluate a pupil cultivates a superordinate schema that henceforth anticipates events to be of that nature. Could it be that teachers who ask 'which is the best scheme?' or 'what's THE way to teach backward readers?' do so as a result of their own schooling and educational experience? Certainly a characteristic feature of educational settings seems to be that they develop, cultivate, transfer and impose on their members schemas or 'cause' maps. Their purpose would seem to be to reduce uncertainty, to provide ready-made interpretations – easy to act upon 'world' views. Such consensually held schemas become anticipatory schemas which can lead to self-fulfilling or self-sustaining prophecies. Reading research which is expected to be 'boring' is highly likely to be boring to that learner; the individual expecting to be interested and fascinated is much more likely in communicative interactions to be stimulated in the manner anticipated. Salomon argues strongly that interaction is reciprocal. He assigns a heavy responsibility to attributors. They are likely to get what they expect!

So are there *specific* teacher schemas which can be changed as the result of the way in which research information is conveyed in in-service education? Or are the characteristics attributed to reading research likely to be related to superordinate schemas that are the result of the learner's educational experience in the past? For me, I shall put my trust in the first view, believing that by expecting my listener to be interested, to be prepared to be intrigued and excited by variety and complexity, the teacher will meet me half way, or even more. But in communication that is interactive and thereby reciprocal, both parties are responsible. We are intimately involved in attributing intent to each other. As the saying goes, beauty is in the eye of the beholder. Therefore, in the context of the UKRA Conference 1985 should we have said not 'does quality count', but rather quality DOES count', and by expecting it we are then more likely to find evidence of it!

References

ANDERSON, R., REYNOLDS, R., SCALLERT, D. and GOETZ, E. (1977) 'Frameworks for comprehending discourse' *American Educational Research Journal*, 14, pp. 367–81.

BOLSTER, A. S. (1983) 'Towards a More Effective Model of Research on Teaching' *Harvard Educational Review*, 53, pp. 294–308.

JOHNSTON, P. H. (1985) 'Understanding Reading Disability: A Case Study Approach' *Harvard Educational Review*, 55, pp. 153–77.

KYRIACOU, C. (1985) 'Conceptualising Research on effective Teaching' *British Journal Educational Psychology*, 55, 148–55.

LAMPERT, M. (1985) 'How Do Teachers Manage to Teach? Perspectives on Problems in Practice' *Harvard Educational Review*, 55, pp. 178–94.

ROSS, L. (1977) 'The Intuitive Psychologist and his Shortcomings; Distortions in the Attribution Process', in L. Berkowitz (ed.) *Advance in Experimental Social Psychology*, vol. 10 (New York: Academic Press).

SALOMON, G. (1981) *Communication and Education – Social and Psychological Interactions* (London: Sage Publications).

Chapter 6

Teachers Learning

Joan Dean

This paper examines the responsibilities of the local education authorities and the schools' responsibilities for seeing that teachers as well as pupils develop and learn (with particular reference to reading and language).

Introduction

The major concern of the 1985 UKRA Conference was the development and improvement of the acquisition of reading skills. People came wanting to learn from speakers and from colleagues, ways in which they could improve their own practice and do more to enable the students for whom they are responsible to acquire and be able to use a wide range of reading skills, using the term in its broadest sense to include everything from the initial skills to complex information technology. And reading is but one aspect of the use of language, and reading skills are acquired and practised in the context of the related language skills of speaking, listening and writing and the para-linguistic skills of communication by movement, gesture and facial expression and our use of the things around us.

Over the past twenty or so years we have seen in schools a shift of emphasis from teaching to learning, recognising that a teacher is successful only when the student learns and that student learning involves each individual in making the learning his own so that he can use it in new situations. This shift also recognises that students learn many things which are not part of the intended learning, including some from teachers and some from fellow students. There is a sense in which all teachers convey a hidden curriculum of ideas and attitudes.

People may differ in their views about methods of teaching and learning and about the way in which students learn, but we are all conscious that the teacher is the key person in the process. If we wish to improve and develop language and reading skills we need to make sure that every teacher is aware of the need to teach them, whatever the subject matter may happen to be. The secondary school mathematics teacher, the sixth form science teacher, the physical education teacher as well as the teacher of the reception class and the remedial teacher are all concerned with language and reading, and so are all their colleagues, although the language may be the language of movement or mathematics or graphic design or Basic or Logo.

While we can expect that those teachers who were trained to teach young children will know something about language development and the teaching of reading from their initial training, it is unlikely that many teachers of older children will have had this experience. One of today's tasks is to ensure that all teachers have knowledge in this important area of work and this means not only encouraging those who are training future teachers of older students to include language work in their courses, but also to provide acceptable learning opportunities for the many teachers who were trained at a time when only infant teachers were expected to know anything about the teaching of reading. This is partly the responsibility of the individual teacher and the school, but it is also a very important part of the responsibility of the LEA.

I therefore want to explore teacher learning, looking at it from the point of view of the language and most particularly the reading curriculum. Much of what I want to say applies to other teacher learning, but in considering language and reading one is automatically looking across the curriculum since these skills are needed in almost every aspect of work. I then want to use as examples some of the work we have been doing in Surrey and generalise from this about the role of the LEA.

Teacher learning

I should like to start the consideration of teacher learning by examining the following questions as they apply to language and reading:

> What do teachers need to know and be able to do?
> What motivates a teacher to learn?
> How does teacher learning take place?
> What is the role in teacher learning of
> > students?
> > peers?
> > senior colleagues in the school?
> What does the school need to do to ensure the development of its teachers?
> What does the LEA need to do to ensure the development of its teachers?

What do teachers need to know and be able to do?

In order to be a good teacher of language and reading you need many skills and some knowledge which has a general application, as well as skills and knowledge related to reading and language learning. In addition, the overall attitudes a teacher or a whole staff take up will affect their success in this area of work.

All of a teacher's work reflects his or her overall philosophy and attitudes and however little a teacher considers these aspects they are still important in terms of what the teacher actually does in the classroom. Successful teachers of reading and language usually convey to their students a confidence that they can and will learn. Such an attitude must grow from previous success, however, which means that the new and inexperienced teacher needs to be supported by the confidence and help of experienced colleagues.

Philosophy and attitudes become explicit in aims and working objectives which are most effective when they are clearly seen. This may mean teaching in terms of specific aims for a given lesson, but it also means using the opportunities which arise and making new opportunities to help the learner achieve the teacher's aim. The charts later on in the chapter show some of the ways in which this can happen.

Aims, philosophy and attitudes are of use only if the teacher has good knowledge of the content of teaching. Teacher education at every level therefore needs to help teachers to acquire the necessary knowledge along with the skill to make aims and objectives explicit and to create and use opportunities for helping students to achieve them.

All that we know about child development and the learning process suggests that to be effective, teaching must take this into account. It is customary for teachers of young children to spend time in initial training studying child development. It is unusual to find the same emphasis placed on development for would-be teachers of older students yet the effects of the developmental process are equally important at the later stages of education when young people are coping with the problems of adolescence.

In addition, all teachers need a range of inter-personal skills which involve the practical use of language and gesture and are a necessary part of all the communication which takes place between teachers and students. In particular a teacher needs the skills of presentation, including exposition, questioning and leading discussion. There is a good deal of evidence to suggest that while most teachers become fairly skilled at exposition, not all become so competent at questioning that it really leads to new learning rather than testing existing learning. The skill of leading discussion is also very variable, with many teachers talking themselves for a high proportion of the time rather than enabling students to practise their use of language.

All teachers also need skill in organising the learning situation so that it is most favourable. This involves observing students and interpreting their behaviour to give information about the learning needs of each and creating an environment in which these needs can be met efficiently. This may involve careful arrangement of the classroom to allow for materials to be easily accessible; arranging materials so that access is easy and progression is clear; recording progress and development and using time so that each student is working as effectively as possible.

Part of the process of providing learning opportunities for

students involves problem solving. There will be learning problems which require analysis; problems arising from the use of time and resources and organisational problems. The teacher needs an attitude that problems can be solved and inventiveness in meeting the problems.

Finally, the good teacher needs to be skilled at evaluation. This means not only observing and evaluating students and their work, but also skill in evaluating the whole range of activity.

If we come more specifically to consideration of the skills involved in language and reading we might include that the teacher needs the following:

1. An understanding of what is involved in communication and the part that language plays in this process.
2. A broad understanding of the way language is acquired and developed and the different uses of language and their effects.
3. A broad idea of the process of reading and what is involved for learners in moving from recognising marks on paper to the transmission of meaning through text.
4. A sufficient understanding of information technology to use it and enable learners to use it as part of normal teaching and learning.
5. Familiarity with relevant methods and materials appropriate for different stages of learning.
6. Awareness of the different skills required in reading different types of material and for different purposes and how they can be developed, particularly within the context of other learning.
7. Skill in judging the difficulty of learning materials and matching methods and materials to learners.
8. Skill in assessing and recording progress.
9. Skill in classroom organisation to ensure optimum learning.
10. Skill in identifying and analysing problems in learning and making provision for them.
11. Skill in introducing books to students and helping them to become enthusiastic readers.

Language learning is involved across not only the curriculum, but throughout the daily lives of students at school and at home. It is, therefore likely that a good deal of learning takes place incidentally, some of it as part of learning in any aspect of school work or indeed in work after school is over. The Bullock Report, *A Language for Life* (1973) speaks of language growing through the interaction of language and experience. Many people who were not effective readers at school become so in a job which demands reading of a certain kind. Some who are effective readers of certain types of text never become enthusiastic readers of fiction or poetry and some quite poor readers become avid readers of fiction. Some part of the teacher's task is to find ways of creating situations in which children want to read.

All teachers of any subject need to be knowledgeable about language skills and reading. So far as the younger children are concerned all aspects of curriculum are involved with the process of learning to use language and to read, and every teacher needs to recognise opportunities for developing these skills.

At the secondary stage there is now much evidence that some of the texts students are offered make unreasonable demands in terms of reading ability. Different subjects make different language demands and a teacher of science, for example, needs to recognise the aspects of work in his subject which form stumbling blocks. An analysis of the contribution of different subjects to reading skills is given later in the chapter.

Older students need the skills which allow them to study independently and these should be developing throughout the years at school and include skills such as observing and questioning as well those of using books. Some older students may have formed bad habits in using text or in listening and the teacher needs to be aware of these and have some idea what to do about them. Many learning difficulties come down to language difficulties in the end.

What motivates a teacher to learn?

People develop their work when they are highly motivated towards it. Part of the task of helping all teachers to become teachers of literacy is that of motivating people whose main knowledge and interest is elsewhere, to learn about and develop skill in the area of language and reading. Most teachers get a good deal of their motivation from interest in the task they are undertaking, especially where others recognise and encourage particular work. A teacher with responsibility for helping colleagues to consider language across the curriculum needs to look for the contributions each person can make or ways in which the work they are doing can be developed to make a greater contribution to the general understanding of language. Teachers who are committed to a joint undertaking with others will feel a commitment to this which may well be motivating and most people are motivated when asked to undertake a particular responsibility. Thus a teacher who is invited to study some aspect of work in reading and language in order to help colleagues will often be well motivated by this.

How does teacher learning take place?

People develop in their work: 1. by personal reading and study; 2. through discussion and work undertaken with colleagues; 3. by observing students and their work and by talking with them about their problems and difficulties; 4. by specific opportunities to observe and question other teachers at work; 5. getting feedback on their own performance from colleagues and students; 6. by experimenting and evaluating; by taping lessons and listening or viewing critically; 7. through experience of particular tasks and specific training opportunities and in many other ways, including in-service courses.

It is important to recognise that adults as well as children need to make learning their own by using it. Teachers as well as children learn better when they are asked to analyse, classify and develop ideas, and act on material rather than taking it in passively. Lectures are limited in their effectiveness and workshop activities are usually more effective for teacher learning when judged by the criterion of their effect on what happens in the classroom.

What is the role in teacher learning of students? peers? senior
colleagues in the school?

We have already noted that feedback on performance plays an
important part in all learning for teachers as well as for
students. Students provide feedback for the teacher all the time
and most teachers are sensitive to the body language clues they
receive as well as sometimes listening to verbal comments.
Students could very often offer more than this if the teacher
could find a way to ask for it. A group asked for comment about
the way part of a lesson went, may be helping themselves as
learners as well as helping the teacher. The teacher is also
demonstrating that we should all use each other to obtain
constructive support.

Similarly peers and staff in senior positions can offer
feedback. They can also offer models and it is important for
inexperienced teachers who are working out their own teaching
style to see a number of other teachers with varying styles at
work. Other teachers can also offer help of many kinds, making
suggestions, sharing ideas and materials and generally
supporting each other.

What does the school need to do to ensure the development of its
teachers?

Ideally a school should have a programme for staff
development which starts by considering the learning needs of
each person when he or she joins the staff. This should include
not only the needs specific to the job the person has been
appointed to do, but consideration of the cross-curriculum
learning needed including knowledge of language and reading
as it applies across the curriculum. The programme is thus
concerned on the one hand with the needs of individual
teachers but also with the needs of the institution as a whole.

The programme might well contain not only straightforward
opportunities to take a course, which might be school-based or
school-focused, but also opportunities to work on specific
problems and activities in which language plays a part.
Teachers might be encouraged to undertake individual reading
and study, to try small pieces of research with their own

students or to join with colleagues in making worksheets and materials, seeing these and many other activities as leading to better knowledge and understanding on their own part of as well as leading to better student learning.

The daily life of an institution offers many opportunities for teacher as well as student learning, providing that those in management are aware of this and use the opportunities which arise. Selecting books for the library could well involve discussion of what makes reading difficult. Making worksheets or providing notices to enable students to work independently also involve a consideration of readability. Provision of material for the least able requires thought about the reading process, and so on. This approach is most effective when members are mutually supportive, open-minded, able to regard criticism objectively and to use it, ready to offer each other a reflection of performance. Specific training opportunities are most likely to be effective when they have been developed as the result of identifying a particular problem and thought about its solution.

A school may draw on people outside in many ways, using the resources of the teachers' centre, the contribution of staff from local colleges, visiting other schools and working with teachers from them and so on. We have also seen recently that parents can make a substantial difference to their children's progress in reading if they are involved. We must also recognise that children will learn language from their parents in the first place.

A programme for staff development needs within it an element of review for individuals and for the whole programme so that teachers can be encouraged to set goals and evaluate their progress towards them.

What does the LEA need to do to ensure the development of its teachers?

The LEA, as the employer of teachers, has a particular responsibility for their development. Its contribution will include not only the LEA course programme and teachers' centre provision but the contributions of the whole range of support services including inspectors and advisers, educational psychologists, speech therapists, and so on. LEA staff offer evaluation, analysis of problems, advice to individuals and groups of teachers, access to collections of books and other materials, etc.

This topic is developed in greater detail in the last section of this chapter (The role of the LEA, p. 73).

Work in Surrey

When I arrived in Surrey in 1972, I shocked my colleagues by declaring that I believed every adviser should be an expert on the teaching of reading. While I have moved a little from this point of view in the light of the many other things in which we need expertise, I still believe that the skills of teaching reading and appropriate knowledge of language should be widespread among teachers and thus among advisers.

In the early 1970s we were able to appoint an inspector, one of whose responsibilities was reading, and we provided a range of courses for primary teachers and for language co-ordinators as well as making good use of the Reading reading centre. This started the process of considering language more widely at the primary stage and, at about the same time, our English inspector was following up the Bullock Report with conferences and working parties on language across the curriculum.

Surrey is fortunate in having a number of centres designed to cater for children of primary school age and average ability, but who are having serious learning difficulties. These centres provided teaching for some children and a certain amount of advice to the schools from which their children came. Some have come to make a very real contribution to work in their area, offering exhibitions of materials, a consultancy service and meetings for teachers at various levels.

Staffing in the early 1970s was comparatively generous and many middle schools in particular had been able to recruit teachers for part-time work with children who had learning difficulties. Secondary schools, for the most part, had their own remedial departments.

In Surrey, as in other authorities, we have suffered from cuts in provision. This initially had the effect for the middle schools of cutting out remedial provision, since a great deal of the work was done by part-timers. This led us to ask questions about how we felt this provision should be made and we concluded that even if we were able to restore some of the staffing and encourage middle schools to appoint remedial teachers, it was still essential at this stage for the class teacher to be knowledgeable about literacy skills and sufficiently well organised to provide for children at different stages of learning. While this was only one part of the overall literacy programme, it was a part which teachers recognised as posing a problem and therefore was a useful starting point for literacy work in the middle school.

We therefore set up a group of inspectors and educational psychologists, one of each from each educational area of the County to consider and support work designed to help middle school teachers. This group has met monthly ever since. The group concluded that the greatest area of need was for help with classroom organisation and we accordingly provided courses on organisation in each area. This led us to consider some larger-scale effort and we started by talking with a group of heads and remedial teachers about how they saw their problems and needs. This resulted in some written material (Surrey Inspectorate, 1982) – a booklet for heads on school organisation, another for classroom teachers and a third for specialist teachers. We also decided to try to run enough conferences in the county to enable every middle school teacher to attend one.

In consultation with heads we agreed that one of the occasional days to which schools were entitled should be used for area conferences to which heads would come, bringing their entire staff. Each conference would be a one-day affair but most of the day would be spent in seminar groups, each studying an aspect of literacy and led by someone expert in the field. We were able to run these conferences for about 200 teachers at a time, with nine or ten seminar groups in each. This allowed each group to work closely together and to ask questions and explore problems. We suggested to the heads that they should send a member of staff to as many of the groups as they could with instructions to take notes for feedback to the entire staff later. There was also a carefully planned exhibition with information about each part of it and time was allowed during the day for each group to visit the exhibition and take notes of what was there.

These conferences were followed up by meetings of heads and other teachers led by the inspector/psychologist team in each area. There was some evaluation of the conferences and each group then planned work for its members. Schools were also asked to arrange staff meetings to discuss the issues raised by the conferences and to report on the outcomes in terms of development. In general, the conferences were held to be very useful and some of the groups are still meeting and discussing some four years later. As a means of reaching a lot of teachers at the same time this appeared to be a very useful way of working. It took just over three years to get round the whole country.

While this was going on other members of the inspectorate and school psychological service were working on other topics. The English inspector was working with a group of teachers to provide the county guidelines on *Language Development and the Teaching of English* (Surrey Education Committee 1985). This, once published, gave rise to a great many activities. There has also been considerable work on developing writing, and we publish annual anthologies of the best work and provide courses for the most gifted writers amongst our secondary school students.

We have now started to consider the needs of secondary schools for remedial work. This is much more difficult because we take the view that all teachers should be concerned with it and this is far from the thinking of many schools, particularly at the present time when secondary teachers are more concerned about other issues. We are trying to encourage the view that each department should have a teacher who is expert in the language needs of the subject, particularly the remedial needs, who would also be concerned with reading levels of subject materials. We also want to see the remedial teachers being available to assist subject teachers dealing with problems of literacy and any particular learning problems inherent in the subject. We have given a lot of thought to the curriculum for the least able and are in the process of producing booklets for different groups of teachers, including the subject specialist (Surrey Inspectorate, 1985).

One of the most interesting ideas which we are considering at the moment has arisen from the modern languages inspectors and English inspectors working together. They are considering, with help from teachers, the possibility of developing language awareness courses for the early years of the secondary school which would provide a background of linguistic ideas for both areas of curriculum. This is at a very early stage but seems to have much to recommend it.

We also have a group of secondary schools working on the Schools Council use of English material and while this hasn't taken off as widely as I had hoped, it has nevertheless been interesting and valuable.

The role of the LEA

All that I have written so far points to their being many ways in which teachers learn and develop in their work. The LEA may foster this development in a whole variety of ways. These might be listed as follows:

Providing courses and conferences This is the straightforward approach, but there are two distinct attitudes that can be taken. You can aim to have as wide a coverage as possible, on the grounds that if a whole staff attend a confence together some of what they learn might stick. Alternatively, you can take the view that work is more profitable with a small, keen group, who then go back and share their learning with colleagues. Both approaches would seem to be needed if it is wished to create an overall climate which is sympathetic to the ends you are seeking to achieve. It is also very important to get head teachers involved, particularly at a primary stage, because we need their support if anything is to happen in the schools.

Working with the staff of a school

Another effective technique is to work with the whole staff of one or two schools. This provides for wide coverage and if the programme has been designed to meet identified problems which concern everyone, teachers are likely to be well motivated. We have done a number of one-day courses of this kind, often with the aim of providing a school scheme of work for some aspect of literacy.

One technique which we have found to be very effective in primary schools is to take an aspect of language work and ask each teacher or year group of teachers to identify five things that they expect children entering their class to be able to do and five that they should be able to do by the time they leave the class. These are then put together for discussion and eventually form a broad statement about what is expected at different stages.

The problem about making provision for work with the staff of one school at a time is that it is time-consuming, but if you gradually train a team of teachers to undertake this work, there can be a multiplier effect. We involve our peripatetic teachers in this work and there have been a number of very good sessions. One particular peripatetic teacher has worked with a number of staffs, helping them to classify and code their books.

Evaluating what is happening

An advisory service can very often help schools and teachers to develop their work by reflecting for them the work currently in progress as it appears to an outsider. This then involves working on how it might be improved or developed further.

The educational psychologist may also

reflect what is happening to individual children and this too is part of the way teachers learn.

In addition, an adviser may help teachers to find ways of helping students in the context of other work. For example, the charts later in the chapter give a framework for considering the different types of reading material which students are encountering. This can be used as it stands or as a blank with only the headings. Teachers then work together to fill in the cells.

Providing learning material for teachers

The right kind of material can be very valuable in helping teachers. It can be material written for particular individuals or material for discussion by groups of teachers. It can be simply text or a mixture of audio and video tape and other materials. It can also be computer-based material.

It is important in providing such material to keep it reasonably brief, to make it as easy to use as possible and to meet problems which teachers are known to experience.

Helping schools to produce programmes and schemes of work for cross-curriculum areas

In the past, although good schools considered and worked on cross-curricular areas such as language, personal and social development and problem solving, very few actually had schemes of work for these areas with a clear idea of how the learning might take place. An advisory service can be helpful to a school in working with the staff to produce documents of this kind and then monitoring the progress of their implementation.

The role of the teacher

The key role of the teacher has been emphasised elsewhere in this paper. The quotation below from *Framework for Reading* (Dean and Nichols, 1972) describes this as follows:

> All consideration of the process of education comes in the end to a consideration of the difficult task of the teacher. Good materials and good equipment will enable a teacher to do a better job, but what happens in the classroom is only as good as the adults there can achieve. This is no sense to deny the fact that many teachers truly enable their children to learn independently and to become agents in their own learning. However, even in these cases, it is the teacher who has created a situation in which this can happen. A wise teacher will work towards this, but the responsibility is in her hands.
>
> What sort of teacher then, is one who enables children to learn to read? We have seen that she is one who believes that they can, and has the ability to instil her confidence into them. We have also seen that she needs to be efficient and well organised, able to use opportunities as they arise.
>
> She must know her materials and be a real expert in matching the material to the child. She also needs to be inventive and create, aware that she may need to find a dozen ways of offering a child the same material so that he may eventually make it his own.
>
> She needs to be intuitive, sensing when a child needs help and quickly aware of the clues which show her that he has not grasped something. At the same time she needs to be analytical, able to break learning down into sufficiently small steps for the slowest learner, while providing challenge for the most able.
>
> Teaching is an art and a science, depending on relationships and feeling on the one hand and a scientific approach to problem solving on the other. Individual teachers will lean in one direction or the other, but to be a truly successful teacher of reading, a person must have the sensitivity of the artist and the analytic ability of the scientist.

Reading for Different Purposes: First Schools

Purpose	Type of material used	Type of language experienced
To acquire/practise reading skills	Reading schemes Early reading books; picture and story books; poems; general information books Teacher-made materials	Language which follows children's speech as far as possible Language for learning to read
To gain enjoyment; develop imagination and extend experience	Picture books; story books; poems; general information books;	Contact with a wide range of vocabulary, language structures, use of language, presentation, etc.
To learn generally or to gain specific information	Information books; story books; simple reference books; encyclopaedias, etc.	Use of specialist vocabulary Information given in different forms of language Narrative offering a different route to information
To follow instructions to do or make something	Work cards and work sheets, both published and teacher-made	Instructional modes of language
To acquire cultural background	Traditional stories; nursery rhymes and jingles; poems, etc.	Traditional language

Reading for Different Purposes: Middle and Secondary Schools

Purpose	Types of material used	Type of language experienced	Areas of curriculum
To develop and practise reading skills	Material from course books, literature, newspapers, etc. It is important to include material with a function in the outside world as well as material designed for children's learning	Should be deliberately varied so that children meet a wide range of language use	All areas involving reading, including out of school activity
To gain enjoyment develop imagination, extend experience	Story books, poetry, information books; material written by the teacher or by other children; newspapers and magazines; historical, geographical accounts; pictorial material	Wide variety including narrative, description, conversation, poetic forms, journalism of various kinds, language from the past and foreign language use	All areas involving reading particularly English; history; geography; social studies; drama; foreign language work
To learn generally or gain specific information	Information books; text books; material written by other children; reference books, including dictionaries, encyclopaedias, story books, newspapers and magazines; documents; forms	Mainly factual material; use of symbols; graphs, charts; tables; plans; maps; newspaper language	History; geography; social environmental studies; science; mathematics
To follow instructions to make or to do something	Work sheets and work cards; material written by other children; instruction kits; e.g. instructions in everyday use, recipes, plans for making something, etc.; common forms	Instructions for work to be done; use of diagrams; filling in forms; mathematical/ scientific language	Mathematics; science; home economics; art and craft
To acquire cultural background	Narrative; poetry; historical accounts; essays; plays; the Bible and other religious writings; biographies; critiques, etc.	Narrative and poetic language; language of other times; biblical language; language of plays; essays	History; religious education; geography; Social/ environmental studies

References

BULLOCK REPORT (1975) *A Language for Life* (London: HMSO).

SURREY INSPECTORATE AND SCHOOL PSYCHOLOGICAL SERVICE (1982) *Remedial Work in the Middle School: School Organisation; Remedial Work in the Middle School: The Classroom Teacher; Remedial Work in the Middle School: The Specialist Teacher.*

SURREY EDUCATION COMMITTEE (1983) *Language Development and the Teaching of English* (Surrey Guidelines) (obtainable from The Media Resources Centre, Glyn House, Ewell, Surrey).

SURREY INSPECTORATE AND SCHOOL PSYCHOLOGICAL SERVICE (In preparation 1985) *Remedial Work in the Secondary School: The Curriculum; Remedial Work in the Second School: School Organisation; Remedial Work in the Secondary School: The Remedial Department; Remedial Work in the Secondary School: The Specialist Teacher; Remedial Work in the Secondary School: The Subject Teacher*

DEAN, J and NICHOLS, R. (1972) *Framework for Reading* (London: Evans (Books) Ltd) (new edn to be published by Bell & Hyman, 1985)

Chapter 7

Teachers of Reading: Planning for the Most Effective Use of Their Time

Vera Southgate

All teachers are eager to help their pupils to learn to read. The majority of teachers work extremely hard at this task. Indeed it is suggested that they usually work far too hard – *using ineffective techniques. Observations in classrooms reveal that, in general, the harder the teacher works in reading periods, the less work their pupils do.*

It is suggested that, if teachers organised more group activities and undertook more advance planning of the tasks which each group would be expected to undertake in reading periods, progress could be greatly accelerated. Practical suggestions are put forward as to exactly how this can be achieved.

Introduction

A recent article in a national newspaper by a teacher who had just completed her first year of teaching (Leader, 1985), illustrates her awareness of the need for guidance about organisation. She writes:

> At college I had been taught to teach. I know Piaget's theory of child development, Chomsky's theory of language development. But I had not been told how to organise a classroom, how to deal with parents, or how to cope with the administration involved in teaching.

While research in the field of reading has shown an enormous increase in recent years – as witnessed by the growing number of research reports listed annually in the British Register of

Reading Research (Bentley and Goodacre, 1976–83) – research reports concerned with classroom organisation and teachers' uses of their own time are noticeably lacking. Yet this is one area of reading research which I consider vital.

Current information on teachers' allocation of their time

Any knowledgeable visitor to British primary schools, for example Her Majesty's Inspectors, local advisers, university and college lecturers, and so on, can testify to the time and energy primary school teachers expend in their efforts to help their pupils to learn to read. That teachers work extremely hard is not in doubt. This being so, it is important that teachers' time and energy should be used in the most effective way possible. Yet few research projects have focused on this important area of teacher-effectiveness.

The Bullock Committee

In the survey undertaken by the Bullock Committee, *A Language For Life* (1975), one of the questions asked was, 'How often does the child read to the teacher during a week? From the teachers' replies, we learned that 'their greatest emphasis was on hearing the poorest achievers read aloud to them'. However, over half the teachers of six-year-olds heard all their children read at least three or four times a week. By the age of nine years, 20 per cent of pupils were still reading aloud to the teacher three or four times a week, while 63 per cent were doing this once or twice a week.

The Bullock Committee's conclusions about teachers' use of their time were as follows:

> There is no one form of organisation of schools, or classes within schools, which will suit all situations.

and

> We believe, however, that the form of organisation best suited to language development is a flexible one in which

independent work by individuals and small groups is the principal form of activity.

Extending beginning reading

As British teachers are now well aware of the main findings of the Schools Council's research project, *Extending Beginning Reading* Southgate *et al.*, (1981), here I shall only summarise briefly, for the benefit of overseas readers, those findings related to teachers' and pupils' use of their time in reading and language periods.

Outline of the project This four-year research project was concerned with pupils aged seven to nine-plus. Investigations into teachers' classroom practices were based on the use of observation schedules and on teachers' logs of reading/writing periods. Additional supporting evidence was gained from large Teachers' Reading Research Groups. All the evidence gathered in these different ways was mutually supportive.

The main findings of the project
1. All teachers of children aged seven to nine-plus gave high priority to the teaching of reading and writing.
2. The time set aside by teachers for reading/writing/langauge activities was devoted mainly to the following activities, in the order given:
    (a) Listening to individual children reading to them from teacher-selected books, while the remainder of the class were engaged (or supposedly engaged) in reading and writing activities based on these same 'teaching books';
    (b) Helping individual children with 'free writing' or 'topic work' by supplying the correct spelling for words requested.
Frequently these two activities ran concurrently, with the teacher supposedly listening to one child reading aloud on her right, while she dealt with queries from a queue of people on her left!
3. In such sessions, which lasted from 20–40 minutes a day, and sometimes a whole hour or more, teachers worked

extremely hard. They were continually switching their attention from the child reading aloud to either the queue of pupils with queries or to other pupils who were misbehaving or failing to get on with the set tasks. In a 20-minute observation period, the average number of attention switches for all teachers was 15: the maximum number for an individual teacher was 32.

4. Consequently, although children may have stood beside a teacher for three or four minutes, merrily reading aloud, the time actually devoted to them by the teacher was extremely brief – on average about thirty second! This, I suggest, is totally useless for any effective tuition.

5. Meanwhile, in such periods, this high energy output of teachers was rarely reflected in concentrated task-orientation on the part of the pupils, who spent, on average, one third of their time on diversionary activities. In some cases children spent two-thirds of their time on activities unrelated to the set tasks. Indeed, in such lessons, there were strong indications of an *obverse* effect on certain pupils – high teacher output being related to low pupil output.

Clearly, such a system of organising teaching–learning activities is not an efficient way of utilising the teacher's time, energy and expertise. Yet, for 25 out of the 33 teachers observed in the intensive study year, this was their sole method of helping to forward children's reading progress. The remaining 8 teachers did some group work, mainly with the better readers.

6. (a) *Basic skills*   With only 4 per cent of reading time devoted to teaching/learning of the basic skills, it is not surprising that children did not do well in these areas.

   (b) *Phonic skills*   We found that only 35 per cent of eight-year-olds and 45 per cent of nine-year-olds knew the common rules in the English language. The fact that nine-year-olds showed the same phonic weaknesses as eight-year-olds, indicated lack of diagnosis on the part of their teachers.

   (c) *Recognition of common sight words*   With regard to the 200 most commonly used words in our language, (McNally and Murray, 1962) only 20 per cent of eight-year-olds and 31 per cent of nine-year-olds recognised them all immediately. Yet we never saw any teacher either test her pupils' recognition of these words or set up practice activities to ensure that the words were mastered.

7. All teachers were eager to promote their pupils' interest in books. They regarded the practice of reading stories aloud to them as the best means of achieving this. In fact, most teachers spent more time on reading aloud to their pupils than the time they set aside for children to read books of their own choice, that is to satisfy the interest aroused and to encourage the habit of reading to become established.

8. Practically no time was devoted to training in the use of dictionaries or reference books, despite the fact that large blocks of time were devoted to 'free writing' and to project work.

Teachers' greatest problem

Teachers' greatest problem is that the older their pupils, the wider will be the range of Reading Ages from 5 to 10 years. While for ten- or eleven-year-olds, the range can be from 6 years to 13 or 14 years.

Let us make no mistake about it – to provide appropriate tuition for thirty-odd children, all at different stages of learning to read, is no simple task. It requires:

1. A knowledge of the reading process, i.e. how children actually do learn to read.
2. Experience in using various assessment techniques.
3. Knowledge of available reading resources and their approximate levels of difficulty.
4. **Great organising ability** – particularly with regard to the most profitable use of their own time. (Unfortunately, students did not enter teacher-training establishments because they were good organisers!)

Teachers themselves are well aware that, with classes of thirty or more pupils, all at different levels of reading ability, there is a great deal to be done in a limited amount of time. They appear to have concluded that individual tuition is the only feasible solution. This is despite the fact that if they divide the available time by the number of pupils in the class, it becomes obvious that individual tuition cannot be a practical proposition. Nevertheless, teachers' general reaction is to push themselves to the limit – flogging themselves to death – trying to listen to individual children reading aloud to them for extremely brief periods, while a considerable proportion of the class is frequently doing little that will forward their reading progress.

What is the solution to the teachers' problem? Teachers have four options for organising her pupils' reading tuition – on an individual basis, a group basis, a class basis or using a combination of all three systems. The Bullock Report (1975) advocated the latter system when they stated:

> We therefore consider the best method of organising reading to be one where the teacher varies the experience between, individual, group and class situations according to the purpose in hand.

I entirely agree with this statement. The Bullock Committee, however, did not spell out how best this might be undertaken.

Planning for the effective use of teachers' time

Requisite skills for effective reading

At any level of reading, provided the reader is motivated to want to read, there are two main requisites before effective reading can take place. They are; first, the reader must be able to identify, on sight, the vast majority of the words in the text; and second, the reader must have one or, preferably, more than one, technique to help him to decipher those words in the text which he does not recognise immediately.

Sight vocabulary   To make sense of a passage of prose, the young reader needs to have immediate recognition of about 99 per cent of the words in the text. (This is the independent level of difficulty.) Consequently, the teacher must be constantly striving to help children to enlarge their sight vocabularies – the store of words they recognise immediately.

Techniques for deciphering unknown words   Until quite recently, teachers tended to assume that the most important, and frequently the only, tactic for deciphering unknown words was to apply phonic rules. When a child was 'stuck', the teacher said, 'Sound it out' – *and many still do.* 'Guessing' was frowned on.

Now, however, mainly due to the work of Frank Smith and Kenneth and Yetta Goodman, we are aware that the text itself provides clues to unknown words. The reader's awareness of the meaning of what he is reading provides him with 'semantic cues' to unfamiliar words. His general awareness of the grammatical structure of our language provides him with 'syntactic cues' to words which, at first sight, he may be unable to decipher. When his phonic skills are *then* brought into action, the child may gain meaning from the word which first puzzled him. Accordingly, when a pupil is reading aloud and fails to recognise a word, the teacher's usual response of 'Sound it out', might well be more helpful to the child if she said, 'What do you think it might be?'

Two important rules for the teacher

Any teacher might well quail at the prospect of attempting to organise all the things which need doing if all her pupils are to be provided with effective reading programmes. Take heart, however, as part of the answer lies in following two important rules:

   RULE 1 THE HARDER *YOU* WORK (IN CLASS) – THE LESS THE CHILDREN WORK!

   RULE 2 NEVER DO ANYTHING YOURSELF WHICH YOU CAN TRAIN SOMEONE ELSE TO DO FOR YOU!

Concentrate on learning rather than teaching

Let us consider Rule 1. The implications of this rule really relate to the importance of advance planning for children's learning (i.e., practice activities). I place children's learning first, rather than teachers' teaching practices as, frequently, the more the teacher concentrates on what she should be doing, the *less* learning is actually taking place.

If teachers are so busy striving to achieve the impossible – and generally unnecessary – goal of 'hearing' every child read aloud to them as many times a week as possible, they will have no time, and little remaining energy, to draw up and put into practice systematic plans for children's learning activities. Whereas, if teachers did nothing else but plan appropriate practice activities for their pupils, in advance, then sit down at the table, with arms folded, and do nothing else but watch the pupils actually getting on with the set tasks, reading progress would increase dramatically.

So, I say to you – Concentrate on *children's learning* rather than on what you should be teaching. Good teaching is really just organising appropriate, successful learning activities.

Learning through practice

Reading practice

We all know the old saying, 'Practice makes perfect' and this is just as true for learning to read as for the acquisition of any other skill. Thus, at the top of my list of priorities for learning to read, I do *not* place the skills which the teacher should be trying to teach her pupils. Rather do I stress, first, the need for children to have plenty of opportunities and encouragement to read quietly to themselves, from self-chosen books, which the teacher knows they will be able to read. This activity alone, if properly organised, will forward children's reading progress much faster than if teachers concentrate on trying to teach them this, that or the other. As long ago as 1972 (Southgate, 1973), at the Annual Convention of the International Reading Association in Detroit, I stated:

> In all reading tuition the first aim should be to produce children and adults who *want* to read and who *do* read: the second aim should be to help them to read effectively. If the second aim is given priority, it is likely that the first aim will never be achieved.

Organising a graded collection of books   The simplest way of ensuring that children do a great deal of personal reading is to provide a large collection of books graded according to difficulty. Such a collection is not only valuable for upper infants and all levels of junior children but also for slower readers in the secondary school.

You may think that setting up such a collection of books will take up a great deal of staff time. Certainly it is a time-consuming exercise, but the major portion of the work need not fall on the teachers. This is one of the occasions when my **Rule 2** should come into effect – Never do anything yourself which you can train someone else to do for you.

In my book, *Children Who Do Read* (1983), I spell out in detail how this exercise may be undertaken, with the help of parents, other adults and the pupils themselves. Teachers will do the initial grading of books, by referring to the various graded book lists now available. Groups of pupils of known Reading Ages will act as 'Assessment Panels' – very good reading practice this is! Adults and older pupils will do the labelling according to a colour-coding system. (See Moon and Moon, *Individualised Reading* produced by the Reading–Language Information Centre, University of Reading.)

Using the graded book collection   The next stage is to initiate the children into the system of uninterrupted reading. The following steps will help to establish a habit which will eventually become a pleasurable activity for all children:

1. Set aside a particular period every day for personal reading – perhaps the end of the morning or afternoon.
2. Ensure that each child has at hand a personally-selected book, at his own difficulty level and, if he has nearly completed it, a second one to hand.
3. On the first occasion, tell the class they will be allowed five or ten minutes to enjoy their books, without anyone interrupting them. (It is important that at first you allow too little rather than too much time.) Talk of it as a special treat rather than a penance. Promise that you won't interrupt them.
4. The teacher should then sit at her table facing the class. She should avoid speaking to anyone – for example, by catching the eye of any child who is not reading and making a gesture to

indicate what he should be doing. (Once the procedure is understood the teacher may also read.)

5. Every effort should be made to establish the pattern that children neither talk nor leave their seats during this period.

6. A notice on the door might read, 'Please do not disturb – children reading'.

7. As children become accustomed to the procedure, gradually increase the length of the period – but never to the point where pupils begin to get restless.

The teacher can be quite certain that, in these periods, her pupils are improving their reading fluency far more than if they were standing at her table to receive a paltry 30 seconds of her attention. The children will also be learning many other things as they read, for example, to read rapidly and fluently, rather than halting at every unknown word; to read for sense and meaning; to 'guess', from the context, the meanings of unknown words, just as adults do, rather than stopping to 'sound out' difficult words.

Records of books read   These children will read large numbers of books in a term. Train them to keep records of the titles, with the dates when they finished each book. These records will afford them great pride. They are also useful for showing to parents who might question why the teacher has not listened to their child reading that week. The teacher's reply of, 'But look how many books he has read for himself this term!' is irrefutable.

Skills practice

One might well ask, 'Is this all there is to helping children to read? Should no teaching be done at all? The answer is that many of the skills of reading are learned by reading. Other skills will benefit from the teachers' guidance and from her organisation of specific practice activities – for those pupils in need of them.

Accordingly, I suggest that the proficient teacher will undertake the following steps:

1. Diagnose children's weaknesses.

2. Provide practice activities to rectify the weaknesses. These

activities can, first, take the form of group games and, later, they will be individual practice activities. Appropriate games and activities are described in *Reading: Teaching For Learning* (Southgate, 1984).
3. Check whether the learning has actually taken place.
4. If the task has been mastered, record the fact.
5. If not, provide further – preferably different – practice activities.
6. Retest.
7. Introduce the next step to a single child or a group of children, (rarely, a whole class), who have been diagnosed as ready for it.

Increasing children's sight vocabulary   As reading continuous prose fluently depends on being able to have instant recognition of 99 per cent of the words in the text, then clearly this necessitates teachers doing all they can to increase children's store of words which they recognise immediately. Well-organised games and activities can quickly increase children's store of 'sight words'. Yet, apart from teacher-controlled practice with infants, using large flash-cards, I rarely see children over the age of six involved in activities designed to enlarge their sight vocabulary on a systematic basis.

(a) *'Interesting' sight words first*   Practice in the quick recognition of words should begin with words which are of interest to the children. With infants, I would begin with the first names of the pupils in the class. Many interesting games can be played with these.

Many individual and group activities for learning sight words involve the use of small packs of cards which children can easily handle. Each card has a single word printed on the front and, where possible, a picture or diagram on the reverse side, together with a code number. Each pack of cards is kept in a small tin box, with a title such as 'Colours', 'Numbers', 'Animals', and so on, and a code-number stuck on the lid.

As the preparation of these cards is a fairly time-consuming business, this is an opportunity for the application of my **Rule**

2: parents coming into the school for, say, one or two afternoons a week, can quickly prepare many such boxes of cards.

Children should first practice the words in any pack in a group game such as 'Pick a Word' or 'Racing' (Southgate, 1984). They can then progress to individual practice. The system I always train children to use for individual practice is as follows:

The child shuffles the pack of cards, then holds them in his left hand with the words uppermost.

Step 1
The child looks at the top word and says to himself what he thinks it is. He then reverses the card to check, by means of the illustration on the back, whether or not he was correct. Train him to say to himself, 'If I was *right* (i.e. correct), I put the card on my *right*. If I was *wrong*, I put the card on my *left*. He then goes through the whole pack in this way, ending with two packs of cards in front of him.

Step 2
For the moment, he ignores the cards on the right, as these represent his successes. He goes through the pack on his left two or three times, saying the words to himself and then checking on the reverse side.

Step 3
After two or three practice runs with the left-hand pack, it is shuffled in with the right-hand pack. Step 1 is repeated and, if necessary, Steps 2 and 3.

Step 4
When the child has twice or thrice, after reshuffling the whole pack, read all the words correctly, he is ready to find a 'tester'.

Still working on the principle of saving a teacher's time, a series of preliminary checks of children's recognition of word packs can be undertaken by people other than the teacher. Parents and older siblings are usually happy to do this. The penultimate check is always undertaken by a '*child tester*' in the same class. Practically every child in the class is an accredited tester at some level, for as soon as he has had his knowledge of any pack of cards checked by the teacher (i.e., the final tester), he becomes an accredited tester himself for that particular pack. I always impress on child testers that pupils should not be passed on to me for the final check until they are certain to recognise every word in the pack.

There is no way in which such a programme of individual and group learning activities can be effective unless a meticulous system of checking and recording is set up. The teacher's record book, with pupils' names in a column down the left-hand side, will have the code numbers from the small boxes of cards at the head of the vertical columns. In this way, recording that a child actually recognises all the words in a pack, is simply a matter of putting a date in the appropriate space.

In addition, pupils can keep their own records of words they can read, by recording them – after they have been tested – in their own small notebooks, under the heading of, 'I can read these words'.

(b) *Key Words to Literacy*   The publication of *Key Words To Literacy* (McNally and Murray, 1962) has been of immense value to teachers. The authors state that the following twelve words form over one quarter of all the running words in both juvenile and adult reading materials:

a	and	he	I	in	is
it	of	that	the	to	was

One hundred words account for over 50 per cent of all printed words. When a further 100 words are added, these 200 words represent over two-thirds of all juvenile reading materials.

It can, therefore, be appreciated that for fluent reading it is essential that children should have instant recognition of these words at as early a stage as possible. Even so, nothing would be more likely to cause young children or failing readers to dislike reading than to *begin* their reading tuition with a heavy programme of discrete words which, in isolation, have neither meaning nor interest for them.

However, once children have practised with small packs of 'interesting' words and had their successes recorded, they will quite happily go on to master the first few packs of *key words*. If the teacher reserves the most exciting group games, for example 'Bingo' or 'Housey-Housey', for these dull words, the children will soon become familiar with them. As such words do not lend themselves to checking devices on the reverse sides, these are ideal packs of words for children to take home to practise with the help of their parents. In *Reading: Teaching For Learning* (Southgate, 1984), I have divided the 200 key words into packs of appropriate sizes, in the order of their utility.

Phonic training　As the results of the most recent survey of reading schemes in use in Great Britain (Grundin, 1980) indicate that about 93 per cent of infant schools use a 'look-and-say' reading scheme as their principal scheme, clearly most teachers think of phonic training as incidental and/or usually based on published supplementary phonic materials.

I have four main reasons for believing that some phonic training should form part of every teachers reading programme:
1. Although many of the words in the English language are irregular, there is still a very large proportion of English words which conform to regular spelling patterns. Wijk (1959) claimed that '90–95% of English words follow certain regular patterns in regard to their spelling and pronunciation.'
2. To learn even one phonic rule almost immediately provides children with a whole new batch of sight words. For example, the rule that when a word begins with 'kn' the 'k' is *always* silent, is a rule which Clymer (1963) describes as one with 100 per cent utility – in other words, it is an invariable rule. Children can thus learn to recognise, in one fell swoop, a whole batch of words such as 'knitting', 'kneel' and 'knife'.
3. A knowledge of phonics can help children to decipher unknown words, in context, by confirming or refuting their predictions based on other contextual clues relating to the meanings of sentences and larger units.
4. A knowledge of phonic rules helps children's spelling.

Consequently, I believe that all children should receive some phonic training and that, wherever possible, it should be based on games and activities. In *Reading: Teaching For Learning* (Southgate, 1984) I have listed many publications which describe such activities.

Vocabulary extension   For children to become proficient readers, as well as being able to express themselves appositely in both the spoken and the written word, we need to be continually encouraging them to be interested in new words and their meanings. This work goes on informally in infant classes but from about the age of seven, we need to give it additional emphasis. One simple system I have used is as follows.

In one corner of the blackboard mark a small oblong headed 'New Words'. When a new and interesting word occurs on any occasion, on the radio or on television, in a book or in children's written work, take a minute or two to discuss it with the class. Then write it in the 'New Words' box. Collecting even one new word a day would be fine. Two or three words a day would be quite sufficient. Last thing every afternoon, children read the new words and add them to the column of 'New Words' in their notebooks. First thing every morning they read the preceding day's words; Friday afternoons and Monday mornings are occasions for reviewing a whole week's 'New Words'.

Organisation of reading time

Teachers' faith in individual tuition

During the past twenty-five years or so a cult seems to have developed, not only in infant classes, but extending to pupils aged nine or ten years, that individual tuition is always best. This has occurred despite the fact that both the Plowden Report (1966) and the Bullock Report (1975) advocated a combination of individual, group and class work. Yet, in the project *Extending Beginning Reading* (Southgate *et al.*, 1981), we still found teachers spending most of their time during reading periods in listening to individual pupils reading aloud to them.

Class, group and individual activities

Let us consider which activities relating to reading lend themselves most appropriately to class, group and individual tuition.

Class work　The following are some of the activities in which the whole class might be involved either for a few minutes or for a longer period:
1. The teacher reading aloud a story or other material.
2. Children's uninterrupted silent reading.
3. Vocabulary extension work – as already mentioned.
4. Introduction to or revision of a phonic rule.
5. Introduction to the school library system.

Group work　Two reports on research relating to group work are of interest here. J. S. Kounin *et al.* (1966) watched and recorded the behaviour of certain emotionally distured children within classes of normal children. They noted that the teachers found to be most successful with disturbed children were also more successful than others with normal children. These were the teachers who managed to *convey an impression of total awareness* of all classroom activity and they had more work involvement and less deviancy from their pupils than did teachers who failed to demonstrate this facility.

M. Sandby-Thomas (1983) investigating the organisation of reading in fourteen classes of six-year-olds, found that pupils taught in classes in which reading was heard in groups achieved higher reading standards than those taught individually. More specifically she concluded that:
1. The instruction time was greater for the group pupils than for the individual pupils.
2. The group pupils were 'heard read' more frequently.
3. Group teachers reinforced the reading lesson by follow-up activities.
4. There was much less interruption in the group reading than with individual reading.

She concluded that '. . . the research suggested that the group approach permits a more effective use of time in the teaching of reading.'

Group tuition　Children whose reading tuition is based on a reading scheme are frequently divided into groups according to the stage they have reached in the scheme. I have found that the best way of working with such a group is for the teacher to sit at her own table, facing the class, who are engaged in prescribed reading tasks. The children in the selected group stand around the table, on which they rest their open books. The teacher, while giving her main attention to this group, is also able to keep an eye on the rest of the class, who will have been trained not to disturb her. Furthermore, the seated pupils will be aware that they are being watched.

The group with the teacher can take turns at reading aloud and discussions will occur about the meaning of the story, as well as the underlying meaning (the 'why?' questions – as opposed to 'what?' and 'where?'). There will be discussions about new words and children will be encouraged to 'predict' or guess new words from the context. Ten minutes or so spent in this way with six or eight pupils can be much more fruitful than one minute spent with each child individually. It is a sociable as well as a teaching–learning occasion and, having participated in it, the children will usually return happily to their seats and be content to continue quietly with follow-up activities prescribed by the teacher.

Individual tuition   On certain occasions, while a whole class is engaged in various prescribed reading activities, the teacher will have the opportunity to spend five minutes more with a number of individual children (instead of merely thirty seconds). These longer contacts, allbeit at less frequent intervals, will offer the teacher the opportunity to diagnose weaknesses, for example in *Key Words To Literacy* or in phonic competencies, and to prescribe appropriate practice activities to overcome them; to carry out a miscue analysis to judge a child's use of contextual cues; to examine his record of books read and to probe his reading interests; to plan with him his future reading activities; and to keep records of his progress so that gradually a personal reading profile for each child will be built up.

Total organisational plans

If we are agreed that effective reading tuition should consist of an amalgamation of class, group and individual activities, then it is quite clear that the organisation of the activities cannot be a haphazard affair. The whole secret of the most advantageous use of both teachers' and pupils' time lies in advance planning.

When I was teaching reading to classes of forty children of junior ages, the class, apart from a few children of very low reading ability whom I taught individually, was divided into three or four sections at different reading levels.

I kept a reading planning notebook in which each double spread represented one day's reading period. It was divided into a grid of five-minute intervals on one axis and four or five reading groups on the other axis. Then, every evening, reviewing the groups to which I had been devoting my attention that day, and the work they and other groups had done on their own, I was able to plan exactly what each group would do the next day and where my attention would be focused at various times. (Sometimes the different groups' programmes were written on the board.)

Whatever the original instructions given to each group, such as 'Read the next story in your book', additional, follow-up activities were always listed, for example:

1. Write down the words in the story which you do not understand.
2. Then list all the words you can find in your book which have 'ch' in them.
3. Then practice your word cards.
4. Then read your own chosen book.

These 'then' instructions are extemely important. Supplementary activities should always be listed whenever children are being directed to work on their own, as they should be discouraged from interrupting the teacher when she is busy with other children. In other words, train your pupils to be self-reliant.

Conclusion

The two most important points to remember are these:

1. There is no way in which a teacher can provide adequate reading tuition for 30 or more pupils, all at different levels of reading ability, unless:

   (a) some class work and some group is arranged;
   (b) the teacher does advance planning for every lesson.

2. If teachers can rid themselves of their 'mother-hen-complex', they will realise that it could well be as important to try to teach children to be self-reliant as it is to teach them to read . . . and both can be taught at the same time!

References

BENTLEY, D. and GOODACRE, E. J. (1976–83) *British Register of Reading Research* nos 1–8 (University of Reading: Centre For The Teaching of Reading).

BULLOCK REPORT (1975) *A Language For Life* (London: H.M.S.O.).

CLYMER, T. (1963) The Utility of Phonic Generalisations', *The Reading Teacher*, vol. 16, no. 4, pp. 252–8.

GRUNDIN, H. U. (1980) 'Reading Schemes', *Reading* vol. 14, no. 1 pp. 5–13.

KOUNIN, J. S., FRIESON, W. and NORTON, A. (1966) 'Managing Emotionally Disturbed Children in Regular Classrooms', *Journal of Educational Psychology*, 57, pp. 1–13.

LEADER, J. (1985) 'Handling The "Enfants Terribles" ', *Daily Telegraph*, 1 July.

McNALLY, J. & MURRAY, W. (1962) *Key Words To Literacy* (London: The Schoolmaster Publishing Co.)

PLOWDEN REPORT (1967) *Children & Their Primary Schools*, vol. 1 (London: H.M.S.O.).

SANDBY-THOMAS, M. (1983) 'The Organisation of Reading and Pupil Attainment', *Journal of Research In Reading*, vol. 6, no. 1, pp. 29–39.

MOON, C. and B. (pub. each year) (Reading: Individualised Reading, University of Reading).

SOUTHGATE, V. (1973) 'The Language Arts In Informal British Primary Schools', *The Reading Teacher*, vol. 26, no. 4, pp. 367–73.

SOUTHGATE, V. (1983) *Children Who Do Read* (London and Basingstoke: Macmillan Education).

SOUTHGATE, V. (1984) *Reading: Teaching For Learning* (London and Basingstoke: Macmillan Education).

SOUTHGATE, V., ARNOLD, H. and JOHNSON, S. (1981) *Extending Beginning Reading* (London: Heinemann Educational for The Schools Council).

WIJK, A. (1959) *Regularized Inglish* (Stockholm: Almquist & Wiksell).

Chapter 8

The Community as a Resource for Reading

Viv Edwards and Angela Redfern

The rapidly changing composition of British schools over the last thirty years has raised a number of issues which are relevant not only for the children of more recent immigrants but for all children. Do we look on the linguistic and cultural diversity which we find in schools as a problem to be solved, or as a resource to be developed? And if we choose the latter course, how should we react to the realities of a curriculum and materials which are strongly monolingual and monocultural? We will argue that although there is a serious shortage of materials which recognise the extent of diversity in British society, it is feasible to develop an approach to and resources for reading by moving our focus from schools to the larger community of which schools are an integral part.

What community

For the majority of children attending British schools, standard English is the exclusive medium of education. The importance attached to the standard is such that most people accept without question the notion of Britain as a monolingual society, and it is easy to overlook the fact that standard English speakers have always been outnumbered by the rest of the population. It has been estimated that speakers of the many regional dialects of English make up at least 90 per cent of the population. By the same token, Welsh and Gaelic speakers have been part of the fabric of British society for hundreds of years, although it is only in very recent times that children in Wales and Scotland have had limited opportunities to learn through the medium of their mother tongue.

However, while Britain has never been either monolingual or monocultural, the extent of linguistic and cultural diversity has greatly increased in the last century. Communities of Irish and Yiddish speakers were established in the late nineteenth century; Italians and Cypriot settlers can be traced back to the inter-war period; in the post-war years, refugees arrived from Poland, the Ukraine and Hungary. The boom economy of the 1950s created a demand for labour which was filled by immigrants from the West Indies, the Indian sub-continent, East Africa and Hong Kong. More recently, significant numbers of refugees from Uganda and Vietnam have settled in Britain (Linguistic Minorities Project, 1985).

The schools' response to diversity

The schools' response to the linguistic diversity of the more recent arrivals was scarcely more positive than the traditional stance towards speakers of regional dialects and Celtic languages. Children were strongly discouraged from using their mother tongues. In some cases this was achieved by sins of omission, and the language of the home was accorded no status in the school situation. In other cases, teachers' comments left children in no doubt as to the value system of the school. Reports of teachers telling children to 'stop jabbering' in their mother tongue have not been uncommon. One head teacher even wrote about suggestions of introducing Gujarati into the curriculum in terms of not starting 'that caper'.

The debate surrounding the education of the children of post-war settlers took off in an atmosphere which was not at all supportive of bilingualism. Much of the research in this area which had been undertaken in the forty years leading up to 1960 had reported that bilingual children performed more poorly in schools than their monolingual peers, scoring lower on the verbal parts of IQ tests and showing more emotional problems. More recently, however, it has been pointed out that many of these studies failed to take into account social class, and whether or not bilingual children were being tested in their dominant language. The climate surrounding bilingualism has changed dramatically in recent years and there is now widespread understanding that recognition of the mother tongue is likely to facilitate, rather than impede, children's educational development.

This more supportive climate of opinion in educational circles has been accompanied by a growth in awareness on the part of the linguistic minority communities themselves. The past fifteen years have seen a mushrooming in the provision of 'supplementary' or 'community' schools. There has also been considerable growth in the availability of mother tongue classes within the mainstream school.

What children bring with them to school

Many myths surround the language experience which children bring with them to the classroom. It is not uncommon, for instance, for a teacher to assume that working-class children 'have no vocabulary', and that their mothers simply don't talk to them. This was clearly the assumption which informed a 1980 campaign involving health visitors, speech therapists and social workers in Birmingham which made contact with mothers in supermarkets and distributed 'Mum, talk to me' stickers to children. And yet research undertaken in this area lends no support at all to this assumption. Tizard and Hughes' (1984) study of four-year-old children at home and in school, for example, showed that differences in language use between working-class and middle-class children in the home setting were very small or absent.

Similar assumptions are made about British Black children. The emphasis is almost always placed on the linguistic skills which children do not have, namely the ability to speak standard English, rather than on the rich oral tradition to which most children of Afro-Caribbean origin have access. This tradition includes folk-tales, verbal duelling, proverbs, rhymes, toasting and dub.

By the same token, little attention is paid to the fact that many children from linguistic minority communities have literacy skills in another language, and sometimes in another script. Substantial numbers of children, especially those who speak Cantonese, Urdu and Bengali, have some facility in reading and writing a language other than English. Even very young children often internalise the skills associated with a particular writing system, like moving along the page from left to right or bottom to top.

For a variety of historical reasons, children tend to be judged in terms of the Anglocentric principles which underlie most school curricula, and are often found to be lacking. The only way to avoid this impasse would seem to be to remind ourselves very firmly of the child-centred philosophy of education to which most teachers at least pay lip service. By starting with the child rather than the assumptions of the traditional curriculum, linguistic and cultural diversity ceases to become a problem and unfolds as a rich resource.

Resources for reading

Catching Them Young: Sex, Race and Class in Children's Fiction (Dixon, J., 1977) is one of several books written about the white, male-dominated, middle-class nature of most reading materials currently available in schools. Some progress has been made in this direction: a growing range of books is now based in urban settings, and departs radically from the suburban-semi-detached-with-garden-and-garage world inhabited by generations of reading-scheme heroes and their two-parent nuclear families. Story books, too, include increasing numbers of ethnic minority characters, though they sometimes fall into the trap of tokenism, so that the minority child merely appears in the background or is forced to rely on the white central figure. Alternatively, they may perpetuate racial stereotypes. The otherwise excellent *Brick Street Boys* by Janet and Allan Ahlberg (1975) for instance, portrays the black boy as good at sport and offers a dream scene in which someone is about to be consumed by cannibals. There are, admittedly, many other books which fall into neither of these traps, but they form none the less only a tiny proportion of all the books which you are likely to find in the school library.

It is important to remember that reading is not an isolated enclave, but an integral part of the school curriculum, both formal and hidden. The Anglocentric flavour of the formal reading materials is all too often reinforced by the audio-visual environment in the school. To what extent do the posters, signs and wall displays reflect the multicultural nature of present day Britain? Which festivals are celebrated? What kinds of music do children hear? What dressing-up clothes are available for children to play with? And what are the contents of the shop or home corner? What adults are seen in authority roles? Is it the case that all teachers are white and most of the dinner ladies are black?

Even more critical, we need to consider the attitudes of teachers. In rare cases, racism is overtly expressed and most of us who have worked in inner city schools will be able to provide examples of inflammatory remarks offered by teachers either in the staff room or in the classroom. More often, though, racism is unconscious. Lowered expectations and the failure, for whatever reason, to confront children taking part in racist name-calling in class or in the playground are just two examples of such unintentional racism, but the effect is no less damaging than that of consciously racist behaviour.

Questions such as these are vitally important in determining how children see themselves within the school. Success depends on a sense of self worth. None of us is likely to make progress in an atmosphere where we feel undervalued and ignored, and it is against this background that we offer some suggestions as to the ways in which significant improvements can be made by investing time in careful thought rather than money in material resources.

Language awareness: an alternative approach

There has been a growing interest in recent years in the concept of 'language awareness'. This is an area in which children are as expert as their teachers. As Michael Raleigh says in the introduction to *The Languages Book* (1981):

> Everyone who reads this knows much more about language than can be put in a book. Everyone has managed the amazing job of learning at least one language – and, when you think about it, you use even *one* language in

so many different ways that even *one* is a lot. So you're the expert; make sure you tell the others what *you* know about language and the way it works.

There are many ways in which the school can help children to develop their language awareness, and a sense of their own skills as language users. Do children know how many languages and dialects are spoken in their own class or in the school as a whole? Has the teacher made any attempt to learn at least some basic phrases in the languages spoken in his or her class? Are number and date charts only in English or do they find themselves side by side with other languages? Do children's names on coat hooks and trays appear only in English script? When visitors come to the school and at parents' events, which languages are used for greetings? Which languages are used for school notices? And which languages are used for sending letters to parents?

Monolingual teachers obviously cannot rely solely on their own resources, but there is no shortage of community support for initiatives in this direction. It is possible to invite adults, or indeed older children, to tell groups of children stories in their mother tongue. Professional writers like Samuel Selvon. James Berry and Grace Hallworth also give school performances. Commercial tapes and records of stories in other languages and dialects can be found, but it is also possible for schools to record their own stories for children to listen to. Michael Rosen (1982) found this a very valuable exercise when he was working as writer in residence at Vauxhall Manor School:

> Elaine's sister Judith had told something like eight or nine Anansi stories on tape – some of which we made into booklets – before it occurred to me that we could lend her a tape-recorder and ask her to record her mother. This she did. Her mother, an 'ordinary' working class woman, is as fine a storyteller as anyone anywhere. You don't have to go to the Brothers Grimm, or to this or that book of Beautiful Tales. Great storytellers are amongst us. If you have some of these stories on tape and play them in school, what happens? The parents' culture becomes part of the curriculum, even if it's for only five minutes at a time. And there was Farah, too, who speaks Punjabi at school and

told me she only really liked books on magnetism, but who
finally let on that her grandmother tells her stories. The
result of that is a tape of an old lady telling an epic in
Punjabi which Farah translated for us.

The development of community links requires careful thought
on the part of the teacher. Many parents' experience of school
makes them reluctant to initiate contact themselves, and to
treat invitations to take part in school activities with a certain
degree of suspicion. In our experience, the schools which enjoy
community participation are those which succeed in opening
channels of communication. This can be done in a number of
ways: home visits before the child starts school or nursery
which allow parents to meet teachers on their own home
ground; notices which invite parents and other members of the
school to feel free to visit; displays which invite inspection and
which are of interest to all members of the community; events
which involve all parents.

Children's writing as a resource

The shortage of reading material in languages and dialects
other than standard English is another stumbling block for
both teachers and children. There are now some stories and
tapes of folk tales available in languages which include Urdu,
Punjabi, Bengali and Greek. (Examples include *The Tiger and
the Woodpecker* produced by the Reading Materials for Minority
Groups Project and available from Middlesex Polytechnic, 14
Chase Side, London N14 5PN; and *Tales from India*, a collection
of five stories and a cassette, available from Mantra Publishing
Ltd., Freepost, London N10 3BR.) Various community
publishing projects have also produced materials in both
regional British and Caribbean dialects. (Information on
community publishing projects may be obtained from the
Federation of Worker Writers and Community Publishers'
Consortium, 16 Cliffsend House, Cowley Estate, London
SW9.) The ILEA English Centre and various specialist
bookshops also promote interesting ethnic minority literature. (A useful source for Asian publications is Soma,

Commonwealth Institute, Kensington High Street, London W8 6NQ; and for Afro-Caribbean publications, New Beacon Books, 26 Stroud Green Road, London N4 3EN.) The limited number of sources of literature of this kind need not, however, be an insurmountable obstacle. Again, the community – this time in the form of the children themselves – can prove a valuable resource for literacy.

Children's writing offers unlimited possibilities for developing awareness of their own and others' language skills. This approach can, in fact, be particularly supportive of children's developing bilingualism or bidialectalism, when taken in conjunction with our rapidly-developing understanding of the language-learning process. There is a growing appreciation that language is learned through a series of approximations to the target, each a little closer than the previous one. Drilling or insistence on a standard English model on the part of the teacher in this situation is as irrelevant for the language-learner as parental exhortation to a three-year-old to say 'saw' not 'seed' when the child is interested in communication, not grammatical accuracy.

See, for instance, on the following pages these two examples of Mona's writing with a 3-month interval between them and accepted as they stood by her teacher.

If we have confidence in children's language-learning abilities and create an atmosphere in which they have ample opportunities for hearing and using a wide range of language, we should be able to accept second-language learning errors in their writing as evidence of the gradual progress towards the target language rather than a problem to be corrected. This is particularly important if we are serious about helping children to develop a sense of themselves as writers, since the acceptance of the child's stage of development is more critical than sometimes arbitrary attempts at correction.

In schools with bilingual children there are also plenty of opportunities for producing books in other languages, or bilingual books. Many schools can confirm the popularity, for example, of books based on photographic records of walks, trips and other school events in which the text has been composed by the children themselves. It requires little extra work to ensure that the text also appears in the languages of the

The big spaceship go fast off to a little spaceship

I wonder why? ✓

I went to the Zoo and I saw some fish
and I saw one fish was jumping.

a flying fish!

bilingual children who take part in these activities. Writing of this kind promotes the idea of bilingualism as an asset and not a problem. The school magazine is another obvious place for developing this positive approach.

Conclusion

We have attempted to show that, in spite of the shortage of commercially published materials reflecting the multilingual and multicultural composition of present-day Britain, it is essential for teachers to find ways of acknowledging this diversity. In ignoring the languages and cultures which are to be found within the school, we create a climate in which children feel undervalued and alienated. In contrast, the acceptance of diversity allows us to move beyond the pathological model in which difference is equated with deficit. It enables us to see bilingualism and bidialectalism not as problems but as valuable skills on which the teacher and children can build together.

We have suggested that the best way forward is to develop the awareness in children of the wide range of linguistic skills which are to be found in any classroom. We have also suggested that where teachers lack the requisite knowledge of the languages and dialects spoken by the children that they teach, that the community of which the school is a part can act as valuable resources for language activities of all sorts.

References

AHLBERG, A. and J. (1975) *Brick Street Boys* (London: Collins).

DIXON, J. (1977) *Catching Them Young: Sex, Race and Class in Children's Fiction* (London: Pluto Press).

LINGUISTIC MINORITIES PROJECT (1985) *The Other Languages of Britain* (London: Routledge & Kegan Paul, 1985).

RALEIGH, M. (1981) *The Languages Book* (available from the ILEA English Centre, Sutherland Street, London SW1).

ROSEN, M. (1982) 'Writer in inner city residence'. In *Becoming Our Own Experts, Studies in language and learning made by the Talk Workshop Group at Vauxhall Manor School 1974–79*, pp. 378–91 (available from the ILEA English Centre – See Raleigh).

Part III

Implications for Classroom Practice (General)

Implications for Classroom Practice (General)

Chapter 9

Extending Involvement with Special Books Using Whole Language Games

Nancy Andrews and Rosemary Salesi

Reading involves making predictions using graphic, syntactic and semantic information, confirming those predictions using information from the same sources, and integrating the information gained with knowledge of the text up to that point as well as with prior knowledge. Whole language games based on children's trade books are designed to focus the reader's attention on meaning and provide opportunities to develop and practice reading strategies which utilise the intuitive language knowledge all language-users have. The task cards, which are the heart of the games, include comprehension questions, synonym substitution, sentence completion and sentence building activities. Participants in the UKRA Conference (1985) developed a whole language game based on the picture book, Jumanji *(1981).*

Two secondary school teachers of English taking a graduate practical in reading found themselves teaching reading to a group of six- and seven-year-old children. Necessity became the mother of invention in their case when, casting about for some way to help the children focus on meaning rather than words, they hit upon the idea of making a game based on one of the children's favourite books, *Where the Wild Things Are* by Maurice Sendak (1963).

That very week in their classroom a forest grew to the ceiling and their room became the world all around. An old sheet stuffed with newspaper turned into a two-metre-tall Wild Thing. The floor became one huge gameboard with construction paper spaces for the path. Tables pushed against the walls became Max's Throne, the boat, and the cave, sites where reading activities took place when a roll of the dice sent a child there.

Whole language games

Whole language games based on children's books were first developed in the early 1970s at Indiana University by Nancy Andrews, LeeAnn Jared and Kathy Allen. Modified and changed to board games later by Andrews, Carolyn Burke and others, the games used in the UKRA Conference 1985 workshop were developed by Drs Andrews and Salesi at the University of Maine. The six games used in the workshop were based on *Ira Sleeps Over* by Bernard Waber (1972), *Blueberries for Sal* by Robert McCloskey (1948), *The Biggest Bear* by Lynd Ward (1952), *Alexander and the Terrible, Horrible, No Good, Very Bad Day* by Judith Viorst (1972), *The Strange Story of the Frog Who Became a Prince* by Elinor Horwitz (1971), and *The Lion, the Witch and the Wardrobe* by C. S. Lewis (1950).

Each game consists of a board, pieces for the players to move, a die or spinner, and several sets of task cards which are colour-coded to the game path. The game is designed to extend the reader's involvement with a particular book and to focus the reader's attention on making sense.

The game reflects the book in several ways. The game board path followed by the players may be a graphic outline of the plot. For example, the path for the game based on *Ira Sleeps Over* zigzags back and forth from one side of the board to the other, depicting Ira's indecision (see Figure 9.1). Ira sits on one side, pondering his dilemma, while the teddy bear patiently waits on the other side. Some of the spaces on Ira's side of the board have question marks. The player who lands on the question space must go back one space because Ira can't make up his mind. Some of the spaces on the teddy bear's side have light bulbs. Players who land on the light bulb spaces may move ahead two spaces because Ira has made a decision. (The directions for playing the game based on *Ira Sleeps Over* are discussed later in this article.)

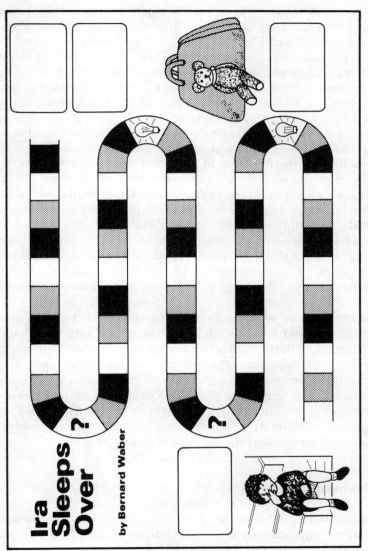

FIGURE 9.1 *Game board based on Ira Sleeps Over*

The game pieces also reflect the story as much as possible, with small wooden boys for *Alexander* plastic teddy bears for *Ira Sleeps Over*, and tiny blueberries and baskets for *Blueberries for Sal*. Play begins with a roll of the die, and as players move their pieces around the board, they land on different coloured spaces which are keyed to various tasks. The task cards are the heart of the whole language games for they are designed to cause the reader to explore in greater depth the book being used. Players must be familiar with a book before they can successfully play a game based on it. A task card may ask the player to find a particular incident in the story, to demonstrate the meaning of a particular word (for example, show how the wild things gnashed their terrible teeth), or to answer a question. Many of the tasks call for the players to use their language strengths to provide synonyms for underlined words, to complete a sentence, to fill a blank with a word or phrase, or to assemble a group of phrases into a sentence. Such tasks reinforce strategies proficient readers use in making sense of what they read. Since no right answers are provided, players often challenge other players, who must use the book to defend answers.

In workshops with teachers such as the UKRA Conference (1985) the participants are encouraged to gain first-hand experience with the games by playing one or more. Discussion during and following the playing of the games provides opportunity to analyse the games in preparation for developing new ones. The workshop group in Reading developed a game based on *Jumanji* by Chris Van Allsburg (1981). Game boards and task card items developed by the group will be used as examples throughout the remainder of this article.

Theoretical basis

When undergraduates in our college courses interviewed children in classrooms in Indiana and Maine, the overwhelming majority of children in the age group of six to eleven years said reading was 'saying the words' or 'knowing the words'. Very few children mentioned making sense or understanding the text, which we believe is the whole point of reading. The games are designed to focus the reader's attention on meaning. They do this in two ways: 1. directly through the use of questions about the text, and 2. indirectly by guiding the reader toward the effective use of semantic and syntactic features of language which can assist in unlocking print and predicting meaning.

Book selection criteria

The choice of a book on which to base a game is very important. Developing a game is a time-consuming task and playing the game often requires rereading a book, sometimes more than once, to check for specific answers or to support interpretations, so the books chosen must be worthy of the attention. Such books are memorable, have lyrical language, use a rich vocabulary and have well-developed characters. In addition, books for games to be used by very young readers may include repeated sentence structures, and novels used to develop games for more mature readers need to have limited numbers of characters, events and sub-plots.

Memorable books should evoke strong emotional responses from readers, should have elements of conflict or tension in the plot, and may also be very funny, suspenseful or have good turn-about endings. These books are often favourites. They may be repeatedly requested for story hour or taken out of the library for home reading.

Since the children will be engaging in activities which require them to re-experience the language of the text, the text should have language that is enjoyable to hear and say, that is, language that is fluid and full of rhythm. The children's level of succesful prediction is high when new words are placed in a meaningful context. A rich text uses both the connotative and denotative meanings of words. Such language will better support the interpretive, cloze and word substitution activities and will promote discussion among the players. Stories from basic readers, Little Golden Books and Walt Disney seldom meet these criteria.

Games developed for use with very young readers may be based on books which use repeated sentence structures such as those called predictable books by Lynn K. Rhodes (1981) and others. This repetition of sentences is very helpful to the beginning reader and helps to ensure focus on meaning because making sensible predictions is easier. Books such as *I Love You, Mouse* by John Graham (1976) and *Where Did My Mother Go?* by Edna Mitchell Preston (1978) work well as they meet the other criteria for memorable books listed above, in addition to using repetitive language.

The characters, even in picture books, should be well developed so that the readers can identify closely with them. If the book has too many characters, the impact of individual characters is lessened and questions for the game are more difficult to create.

Using novels to develop whole language games adds some special problems. As the text increases in length the story may also become more complex, with increased number of characters, sub-plots, events and settings. It is advisable to select novels that have a limited number of characters and sub-plots. *The Indian in the Cupboard* (Banks, 1980), *Tales of a Fourth Grade Nothing* (Blume, 1972), and *Island of the Blue Dolphins* (O'Dell, 1960) are examples of books where the number of major characters is small. If a novel is selected which has a large cast of characters and many events placed in several detailed settings, such as *The Lion, the Witch and the Wardrobe*, (C. S. Lewis, 1961) tasks should be focused around only the main events and major characters.

Jumanji (Van Allsburg, 1981) is a powerful story built around the playing of the board game, '*Jumanji*, A Jungle Adventure Game'. Judy and Peter find a box containing the game under a tree in the park. A note on the box cautions them to read all of the directions before playing the game and the directions state that whoever plays the game must finish it. The children find that with each throw of the die some terrible jungle adventure happens: a lion attacks Peter, a volcano erupts in the living room, monkeys steal food in the kitchen and rhinos stampede through the house crushing the furniture. Judy finally ends the terrifying game by reaching the golden city of Jumanji and shouting, 'Jumanji!' Greatly relieved, the children race from their once-again normal house to put the game back under the tree in the park. The game is finished, but the story is not, as Van Allsburg includes a delightful twist at the end.

The picture book, *Jumanji*, was selected because of its strong plot line, suspense, twist in the ending and the well-written text which includes a variety of sentence structures, rich vocabulary and vivid descriptions. The characters of Judy and Peter are clearly delineated and developed: Peter's somewhat flippant attitude turns to a strong resolve as the situation becomes more critical.

Designing the game board

Once the book is chosen, the next step is the design of the game board itself. The path to be followed by the players can reflect the plot line, as suggested above, or may reflect the book in another way, since many children's books have rather circular plots. A path for a game based on *Island of the Blue Dolphins* (O'Dell, 1960) might be in the shape of a dolphin, outlining the island, for example. The group working on *Jumanji* designed six different gameboards, even though the board for the game in the book is clearly pictured and might be used as it is. Two of the boards developed at the UKRA workshop in Reading are shown below (see Figure 9.2). Both attempt to depict the whole book rather than focusing only on the game within the book. Both end with a question, as does the book.

Game board A illustrates the circular nature of the action, which begins and ends in the park. The first part of the path is plain to reflect the children's boredom in the first part of the story. Once the 'Jumanji' game is found, action picks up, and a roll of the die results in a task to be done. The questions (where the game came from, what the next finders of the game will do with it) are implicit in the 'Q' shape of the whole path as well as in the question mark at the end.

Game board B is a bit more complex. It also illustrates the boredom of the children in the beginning, but the upward slant of the path once the 'Jumanji' game is set up conveys the increasing tension until the golden city of Jumanji is reached. Release of the tension shows in the rather straight slide back to the park, where the upturn in the path and the question mark

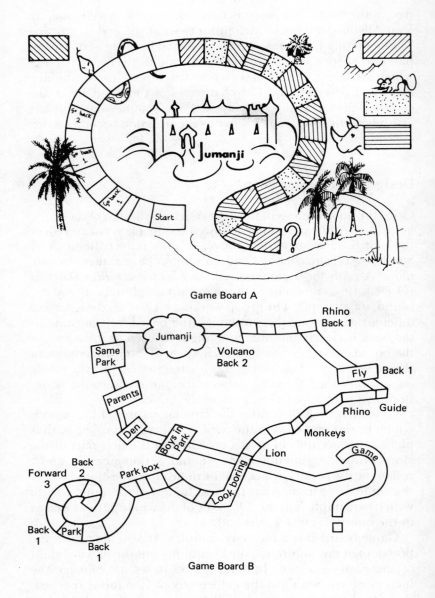

Game Board A

Game Board B

FIGURE 9.2 *Two game boards developed for* Jumanji

both symbolise the new tension which is generated by the starting-over-again ending of the story.

The task cards

The task cards are the most important part of the games and most clearly reflect the theoretical understanding of reading of the person who develops a game. They are what make the games we are discussing whole language games. Tasks in whole language games are designed to reinforce reading strategies which focus on meaning and utilise the intuitive language knowledge all readers have. The chart shown in Figure 9.3 is adapted from Goodman and Burke (1980, p. 35).

Reading involves making predictions using graphic, syntactic, and semantic information, confirming those predictions using information from the same sources, and integrating the information gained with knowledge of the text up to that point as well as with prior knowledge.

Tasks which focus the reader's attention on the graphic system also make use of the syntactic (grammatical) and semantic systems of language since all tasks involve complete sentences. A cloze procedure may be used with one graphic cue given: the first letter of the missing word. The player must fill in the blank space with a word that not only makes sense and is grammatically acceptable but also *begins with the letter given*. Examples from the *Jumanji* game include: 'Mrs Budwing's sons never r...... instructions' (possible answers might be: read, remembered, reviewed) and 'The python s...... into camp' (sneaked, slid, slithered, etc.). If no graphic cue is given in cloze tasks, the reader's options are, of course, much broader. In the first example given above, if no graphic cue had been given, the reader might have responded, 'Mrs Budwing's sons never *paid any attention to* instructions' or 'Mrs Budwing's sons never *heeded* instructions'. Either response would have been correct even though the one in the book is 'read'.

In synonym substitution tasks, the leader uses both the syntactic and semantic cue systems to substitute a word or phrase for an underlined word in the sentence given. One suggestion for the *Jumanji* game was 'Judy heard a faint buzzing

Sources of Cues Emphasised

Reading Strategy	Graphophonic	Syntactic	Semantic
PREDICTING	Cloze procedure with one graphic cue. Example: Max c..... the wild things.	Cloze procedure with no graphic cues. Example: Max ..... the wild things. Synonym substitution: Example: The wild things *gnashed* their terrible teeth.	SAME Sentence completion: Example: The wild things ...... Sentence building: Example: lying on the piano/there was a lion/staring at Peter/and/licking his lips
CONFIRMING	Checking responses: Does the word used begin with the letter that was given?	Checking responses: Does that sound like language? Does it fit the language of this story?	Checking cloze responses: Does it make sense? Does it fit the story? Checking sentence completion: SAME QUESTIONS
INTEGRATING			Comprehension questions. Comparing book to other materials. Writing to a character. Writing from one character to another. Finding things in the book. Acting out parts of the story or characters. Drawing responses or maps.

noise and *watched* a small insect land on Peter's nose.' The player might substitute 'saw', 'looked at', 'observed', 'noticed', etc. Words selected for underlining for synonym substitution tasks or for omitting in cloze procedures should *always* be words for which several possible answers are immediately obvious to the person developing the game.

Sentence completion and sentence building tasks force the reader to use both the syntactic and semantic systems, for the sentences produced must be grammatically correct and make sense. Sentence completion tasks provide the first part of a sentence, which the player must complete. The sentence portion given must not be a complete sentence itself, but must stop at a point that demands finishing, that is, after a preposition or an article, etc. One example developed for the *Jumanji* game is: 'Judy sat down, nervously eyeing the eight-foot snake that . . .'.

Sentence-building tasks provide the player with several narrow strips of paper with phrases on them which can be put together to form a sentence. When these phrases sets are well-designed, the players may be able to put them together in more than one way. For example, these phrases for *Jumanji*: 'lying on the piano/there was a lion/staring at Peter/and/licking his lips', can be put together in at least two other ways: 'There was a lion lying on the piano staring at Peter and licking his lips' and 'Lying on the piano there was a lion licking his lips and staring at Peter'. Thus, at least three different sentences can be made, including the original order of phrases shown above. Sentences for the sentence-building tasks need to have three or more phrases, and it should be possible for the players to put them together in more than one way. (In some games a player may move ahead an extra space for each different sentence made.) When dividing sentences for sentence-building task cards we use the following guidelines:

(a) use capital letters only for proper names and the pronoun 'I';
(b) use no punctuation except apostrophes and commas between words in a series;
(c) use the conjunction 'and' as a single word sometimes to provide greater leeway in constructing sentences;
(d) avoid breaking apart words in series.

The tasks thus far described reinforce reading strategies such as making predictions based on semantic and syntactic information, and dealing with unknown words by substituting synonyms. Each task response can be checked by asking such questions as 'Does that [answer] make sense?' 'Does it fit with the story?' These questions are the basic confirming strategy questions. The tasks focus on meaning somewhat indirectly.

The more direct focus on meaning comes from the question cards. The questions asked should be of different types and may call for responses other than simply spoken answers. At the simplest level, they may call for the reader to find something in the book or to demonstrate the meaning of a word or phrase. At a more complex level, comprehension tasks may ask the player to compare the story with another, to tell what the story reminds him or her of, or to tell what might happen *after* this story to one of the characters. This last activity is especially appropriate for *Jumanji*. Some comprehension activities based on *Jumanji* are: 'Who or what might have left the game in the park?'; 'How was Judy feeling when she begged, "Please, please," as she shook the die?'; 'What evidence was there that the children had not just dreamed about the game?'; 'Say, "Gosh, how exciting" in an unexcited voice'.

Comprehension activities may also push the players beyond the book by asking them to draw maps, pictures, etc.; to act out parts of the story; to respond to a particular situation as one of the characters might; or to write a letter or memo from or to one of the characters. Such activities allow players to respond to the book in other modes, but should be used judiciously as they do require more time than other types of activities. They may, however, be very useful to continue involvement with the game and book over several days if that seems desirable. Whatever the format of the comprehension activity, the best activities are those that result in thoughtful discussion among the players.

Designing instructions for the game

Just as in the game in *Jumanji*, every game needs clear, concise directions. Because the game board design itself effects some of

IRA SLEEPS OVER

by Bernard Waber

Game by Rosemary Salesi and Nancy Andrews

How to play

1. All players must read the book *Ira Sleeps Over*, by Bernard Waber.

2. Two to six players may play. Place game cards on their colours face down on the game board. Each player choose a marker.

3. Throw the die to see which person is first. The highest number is first. If there is a tie, those two players throw again to see who has the highest number.

4. Begin at Ira. Throw the die to determine how many spaces you move.

5. Pick the top card in the stack that has the same colour as the space on which you land.

6. Read the question and answer the card. The other players decide if you answered it correctly. Use the book to check your answers. If you are wrong, go back to the space where you were before this throw.

7. If you land on a '?', Ira can't decide, so go back *one* space and answer the question. If you land on a ⌯, Ira decided, so go ahead *two* spaces and answer the question.

8. The first player to get to the end wins.

How to answer cards

Pink cards . . . . .Answer or do what the card requests. Use the book to check your answers.

Green Pockets . . . .Put the phrases on the strips in order to make a sentence. If you can, arrange the strips to make another sentence that sound right, you may go ahead one more space.

Yellow Cards . . . . .Substitute a word (synonym) or phrase that means the same or nearly the same as the underlined word. If you can give *2* different words or phrases, move ahead another space.

Blue Cards . . . . . . .Finish the sentence so it sounds like it might be found in the book.

FIGURE 9.4 *Directions for the game based on* Ira Sleeps Over

the specifics included in the directions, we will limit the discussion to those general items that should be addressed in developing any game. Directions for any game need to include:
1. Numbers of players.
2. How to set up the game board.
3. Where to start and the direction to move.
4. How to choose the first player.
5. How to move and what to do when landing.
6. How to complete the tasks or answer the questions.
7. What to do if the other players challenge a response.
8. How the winner is determined.

The directions for the game based on *Ira Sleeps Over* are given in Figure 9.4. You may wish to compare it to the game board illustrated in Figure 9.1.

Conclusion

Whole language games based on children's books are designed to enhance readers' comprehension by guiding them back into a special book, and by helping them experience and think about the story in a different way. We certainly would not want or need a game based on every book we and our students enjoy. A few games based on good books can be a welcome addition to a classroom library and allow for the development and practice of strategies for proficient and enjoyable reading.

References

BANKS, L. R. (1980) *The Indian in the Cupboard* (New York: Doubleday).

BLUME, J. (1972) Ill. Roy Doty. *Tales of a Fourth Grade Nothing* (New York: Dutton).

GOODMAN, Y. and BURKE, C. (1980) *Reading Strategies: Focus on Comprehension.* (New York: Holt, Rinehart & Winston).

GRAHAM. J. (1976) Ill. Tomie de Paolo. *I Love You, Mouse* (New York: Harcourt Brace Jovanovich).

HORWITZ, E. (1971) Ill. John Heinly. *The Strange Story of the Frog Who Became a Prince* (New York: Delacorte Press).

LEWIS, C. S. (1961) *The Lion, the Witch and the Wardrobe* (New York: Macmillan).

McCLOSKEY, R. (1948) *Blueberries for Sal* (New York: Viking).

O'DELL, S. (1960) *Island of the Blue Dolphins* (Boston: Houghton Mifflin).

PRESTON, E. M. (1978) Ill. by Chris Conover *Where Did My Mother Go?* (New York: Four Winds Press).

RHODES, L. K. (1981) 'I Can Read! Predictable Books as Resources for Reading and Writing Instruction', *The Reading Teacher*, vol. 38, February, pp. 511–18.

SENDAK, M. (1963). *Where the Wild Things Are* (New York: Harper).

VAN ALLSBURG, C. (1981) *Jumanji* (Boston: Houghton Mifflin).

VIORST, J. (1972) Ill. Roy Crùz. *Alexander and the Terrible, Horrible, No Good, Very Bad Day* (New York: Atheneum).

WABER, B. (1972) *Ira Sleeps Over* (Boston: Houghton Mifflin).

WARD, L. (1952) *The Biggest Bear* (Boston: Houghton Mifflin).

Chapter 10

Representing Comprehension

Sue Sheldon

This paper explores the idea that introducing the iconic communication mode to children through the technique of modelling will reduce the number of reading failures and increase a child's willingness to reflect on what is read. Practical ways of teaching and testing comprehension using this technique are described in the light of a major research study.

During a child's first few years of life, the way they demonstrate an understanding of spoken and written material gradually develops through different communication modes. A parent's teaching may begin by showing the child how to respond to a particular gesture, and success is measured by the child's physical demonstration that they have understood. For example, the six-month-old daughter of a friend of mine responded to the family cat by smiling and pointing. Once she was introduced to paper and books, she soon began to recognise pictures or drawings of cats by pointing. From this gentle introduction to the naming of objects and shapes and the idea that one thing can stand for another, she will soon be faced with the fact that there is another way of representing the concept of 'cat' – black marks on a page.

A categorisation of these modes of communication was first offered by Jerome Bruner (1966). This is how he put it:

> We can talk of three ways in which somebody 'knows' something: through doing it, through a picture or image of it, and through some such symbolic means as language.

For convenience these modes are called *enactive* (acting out, or using gestures to re-enact), *iconic* (using pictures, images, diagrams, etc.) and *symbolic* (using signs and symbols as in mathematics or using verbal symbols as in spoken or written language).

Throughout our lives, we will at some time or another use all three modes, combining them to suit our purposes in gaining, using and communicating ideas. By learning how to operate these symbol systems to translate and reflect on ideas which come from a wide variety of sources, we increase our effectiveness in society. Many children make the transition through these modes of communication without difficulty, whilst many more require some help in moving from the concrete to the abstract; the enactive and iconic to the symbolic.

As teachers, we are continually on the look-out for ways of contributing to our students' ability to extract and communicate their understanding of what they read. Developing the technique of modelling (Merritt *et al.*, 1977), which is based on the iconic communication mode, is one effective way of doing this. This technique is known as mapping in the United States (Davidson, 1982). For some time now, it has been understood that our view of reading will inform the way in which we teach it:

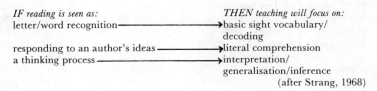

IF reading is seen as:
letter/word recognition————————→*THEN teaching will focus on:* basic sight vocabulary/ decoding

responding to an author's ideas ————→literal comprehension
a thinking process ——————————→interpretation/ generalisation/inference
(after Strang, 1968)

Only recently have we begun to take seriously the challenge set out by Eric Lunzer and Keith Gardner's research (1979, 1984) to encourage reflective thinking; those invisible qualities which help us to learn and communicate.

This paper will explore ways of using diagrams (the iconic mode) as a technique for helping readers to express their comprehension and to develop their ability to discuss their ideas. The technique requires the reader to visually map out some of the ideas conveyed in a passage after first reading it through silently. If the teacher feels that this is asking too much of the reader, it is possible to read the passage aloud or offer a selection of diagrams from which the reader can choose the one

My house faces north and is on a road that runs east and west. To get to school I need to turn left out of my front gate, walk along until I get to the pedestrian crossing, cross the street, turn left and carry along down the road to the first street to the right. Down past three houses is my school.

(*Map*)

Five children went to the green grocers to get some fruit. Jill bought apples, oranges and bananas. John bought pears, apples, bananas and plums. Beth bought oranges, pears and apples. Barbara bought grapes, pears, oranges and a melon. Peter bought only one apple.

(*Matrix*)

My grandparents had three children: Don, Mary and Ted. Only Mary and Ted (my father) had children. Mary had two children (my cousins) and Ted had three children. My oldest cousin just had a baby girl this summer.

(*Hierarchy tree diagram*)

When the sun shines on the sea the water gets warm. Some tiny drops of water rise up to the sky as clouds. Winds blow the clouds over the land. The drops of water fall onto the land as rain. Some water soaks into the ground, some is trapped and stored for us to use. Some goes into the rivers. Most of the water finds its way back into the sea through rivers and drains. There the process begins again. It never stops. We call this a 'cycle'.

(*Diagram*)

I am nine years old, and I was born in 1977. When I was two years old, my sister was born. Then our family moved to a different town in 1981, where we lived for two years. My brother was born in 1983. We moved to our present house after he was born.

(*Time line*)

There are seven rooms in the school. At nine o'clock this morning, some of the rooms were cooler than others. In class A it was 12°C, in class B it was 11°C, class C had 14°C, class D had 9°C, class E had 8°C, class F had 8°C, and class G had 11°C.

(*Bar chart*)

This morning at nine o'clock when we took all of the room temperatures, we found that the coldest room was 8°C. The caretaker decided to record the temperature of the room each hour of the day. At 10 o'clock it was 9°C. At 11 o'clock it was 12°C. At 12 o'clock it was 14°C. At 1 o'clock it was 15°C. At 2 o'clock it was 16°C. At 3 o'clock it was 15°C.

(*Line graph*)

The children from our school travel in three different ways. They come by train, by bus and by foot. Half of them come by foot, 20 per cent come by bus and 30 per cent come by train.

(*Pie chart*)

To make a cup of tea it is important to do things in the correct order. First, put the kettle on. While the kettle is heating, put the tea in the pot. Pour some milk into a cup. Finally, pour the tea into the cup.

(*List or time line*)

Every member of the class plays cricket or tennis. Some of the children play both cricket and tennis.

(*Venn diagram*)

which most accurately represents the ideas from the passage (see Figure 10.1, p. 132). In this way, readers are introduced to the idea that information gained from printed language can be translated and communicated in more than one way. Through looking at examples of various diagrams and how they relate to different texts, readers will get a clearer idea of how to create them for themselves.

Once a reader is a competent decoder, the technique can be used to develop comprehension and generate discussion, for fluent reading is only half way to mastered reading. First of all, it may be useful to identify a variety of iconic formats which are already familiar to schoolchildren. The ten paragraphs in Table 10.1 provide a start in identifying different ways of representing information, for each one can be represented by a different type of diagram or model. If you were to give this selection to children, you would find that most of them would draw pictures of the various elements contained within the paragraphs unless they had already had some experience of modelling their ideas. It is quite important to wean them away from this tendency, for it detracts from the overall concepts and narrows the focus to isolated bits of information. But do keep your eyes open for any indication that the reader does not actually understand the vocabulary of a passage. For example, an American child drew two pictures for the final paragraph: an insect and a ball! Such misunderstandings will take their toll on a child's ability to make sense of reading. You will also find

FIGURE 10.1   *Choosing the best model*

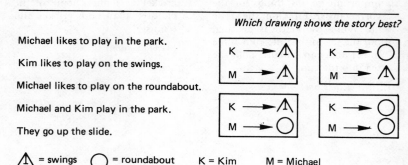

Which drawing shows the story best?

Michael likes to play in the park.

Kim likes to play on the swings.

Michael likes to play on the roundabout.

Michael and Kim play in the park.

They go up the slide.

⚠ = swings   ◯ = roundabout   K = Kim   M = Michael

A big dog sat by his kennel.

He had a big bone in his mouth.

A little dog sat by his kennel.

He had a little bone in his mouth.

Which drawing shows the story best?

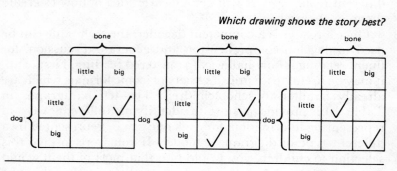

that children working in pairs will create a greater variety of diagrams and will generate more interesting discussion. To ensure that this happens, the record sheet in Figure 10.2 will help.

To use this record sheet, the readers first choose a passage and work together to create an appropriate model. Having done this, they give the finished model to another pair of readers who fill in the evaluation section of the record sheet. These completed sheets can be kept in a file or ring-binder for

FIGURE 10.2   *Models   record   sheet*

Name ....

Partner ....

Purpose ....

Model

	Yes	No
Does the model answer the reading purpose?		
Is the type of model appropriate?		

What points (if any) were left out?

....

....

Were any extra points found by reading between the lines?

....

other children to refer to in order to gain a wider range of ideas for discussion.

It is helpful for the teacher to do some preparation before starting such an activity in the classroom. First of all, not every text lends itself to this activity, so it is important to select a few passages from which the readers can choose. In doing this, you will begin to see that the basic content of the text will put limits on the way it can be represented (see Table 10.2). This table, although not exhaustive, may help to narrow down the range of

TABLE 10.2

Kind of structuring required	Appropriate model
Describing (concerning just the attributes of an object, situation, etc.)	Sketch or diagram (possibly with labels)
Classifying (sorting into groups)	Topic web, Venn diagram, tree diagram, attributes matrix
Comparing (showing similarities and differences)	Bar chart, attributes matrix, preference matrix, Venn diagram, pie chart
Ordering (arranging in sequence)	Time line, ordered list, network, flow chart
Positioning (locating in space)	Scale model, map, scale drawing, plan
Interrelating (co-ordinating similarities)	Table, histogram, scatter graph, graph, Venn diagram

(Graham *et al.*, 1980)

formats which are suitable for representing a particular type of text. These types of representations are illustrated in Figure 10.3. Previous research (Sheldon, 1984) indicated that using this technique with a wide ability range of eight- to nine-year-olds significantly improved the comprehension performance of poor readers, and it increased the time all readers were prepared to spend on the task of reading. They were learning *how* to become reflective readers; a skill which is seldom taught.

In examining the test results from that research, it became clear that the type of testing technique used had an influence on the performance of the reader. That is, poor readers often performed markedly better on some 'reading comprehension' tasks than on others. Perhaps we are actually limiting a child's potential performance through our choice of tests. Tests of comprehension tend to use one technique only, yet performance on each is taken to indicate overall ability in reading comprehension. It is not unreasonable to assume that performance is more a reflection of mastering the technique than of grasping the meaning of a passage. It would appear that when tests are limited to a single technique, and when test

FIGURE 10.3 *Ways of representing ideas*

An *inclusive* model shows that certain ideas or things are the same as each other; they can be shown together in a circle, as in a Venn diagram.

blue
red
green
colours

An *exclusive* model shows that things are different from each other in some way.

carrot
turnip
potato

lettuce
rhubarb
peas

grow under soil   grow above soil

An *intersecting* model shows how some things are different yet with parts the same.

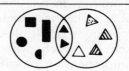

A *hierarchical* model shows the order of importance of things – how they are arranged.

▲ head teacher
▲ ▲ deputy heads
▲ ▲ ▲ heads of year
▲ ▲ ▲ ▲ ▲ class teachers

There are many kinds of *mathematical* models, including graphs and histograms of all types.

height

time
growth of a seedling

A *temporal* model is usually a time line showing how events can be arranged in a linear way.

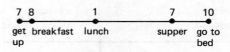

7 8   1   7   10
get up   breakfast   lunch   supper   go to bed

A *spatial* model is a form of map or plan.

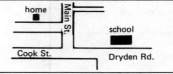

home
Main St.
school
Cook St.
Dryden Rd.

design and construction are unclear as to what aspect of comprehension is being tested, their diagnostic value will be limited.

In order to use a test for diagnostic teaching, the objectives for each item and section should be clearly identified, distinguishing between the stated aspects of ability it purports to measure in order to inform teaching practise. Using a variety of techniques for testing reading will provide children with a broader opportunity to express their comprehension. To investigate the question of whether all aspects of reading can best be assessed by a single technique, I devised a test designed to indicate more specifically the relative effectiveness of testing techniques in relation to the abilities being tested (Sheldon, 1982). This test included items representing three testing techniques (multiple-choice questions, cloze and diagrams), each of which was intended to assess three aspects of comprehension (vocabulary, literal and inferential). Perhaps the pattern of scores would throw light on the relative sensitivities of the techniques to the three aspects of comprehension (see Table 10.3).

TABLE 10.3   *Test design*

Testing Techniques \ Aspects of Comprehension	Vocabulary	Literal	Inferential
Multiple-choice questions			
Cloze			
Diagrams			

Correspondence between items in terms of technique (regardless of the aspect of comprehension tested) emerged only for cloze. As for consistency in performance related to the aspect of comprehension being tested, vocabulary emerged as being consistent, regardless of the technique used to assess it. As a result of the factor analysis, it was clear that the testing *technique* had a greater influence on performance than the *aspect* of comprehension being tested. The major findings from that study (Sheldon, 1982) indicated that vocabulary can be equally satisfactorily assessed by all three testing techniques, that vocabulary can be seen as a separable aspect of reading comprehension (but not literal or inferential comprehension) and that cloze technique does not discriminate between any of the aspects of comprehension.

What can we learn from studies such as this? First of all, that any emphasis on testing is dangerous inasmuch as it tends to encourage 'teaching for tests'. However, getting away from single-mode stereotypes can only help broaden our view both of comprehension itself and how to assess it. Just as purpose in reading is important, purpose in testing is equally so:

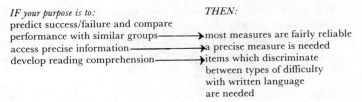

IF your purpose is to:
predict success/failure and compare
performance with similar groups ——→ most measures are fairly reliable
access precise information ——→ a precise measure is needed
develop reading comprehension ——→ items which discriminate
between types of difficulty
with written language
are needed

THEN:

Recently, *The Sunday Times* published an article which described new types of tests which are being introduced in the United States – 'basic skills tests' for school leavers. These tests combine verbal with iconic symbols in an attempt to 'measure the minimum skills and capabilities that are required of adults in order to function adequately in modern society' (Wilby, 1978). In the reading test, for example, children have to answer questions to show that they understand recipes, advertisements, tax forms, airline safety regulations and operating instructions for coffee machines.

Peter Wilby predicted that such tests would meet bitter opposition from British teachers because they fear that far from improving standards, the tests would actually depress them. 'Standards of what?' we might ask. It seems more a question of the way in which judgements about a person's literacy are made. If your concern is about competent functioning in society, then it would be appropriate to look carefully at the way such competence is evaluated. By 1984, the British Associated Examining Board (AEB) had developed 'basic tests' in arithmetic, English and life skills which were designed to assess transferable skills to enable young people to make the most of future training, education and employment. In January 1985 the Secretary General of the AEB wrote to all head teachers about the development of two new areas for examining: computer awareness and graphicacy. There, the test in graphicacy was described as 'the ability to communicate in graphic form'.

The philosophy behind such tests is that success in them can be achieved by a variety of learning experiences and not only through following a traditional course of literacy instruction. So what, now, of our concern for standards? Feedback has already come in from various employers:

> If only we could have applicants capable of passing these tests, we would be very happy. Unfortunately, the applicants we are receiving at present fall far short of these standards. (Scunthorpe, Glanford and Gainsborough Chamber of Commerce)

> Tests of the kind the AEB are developing in graphicacy would provide key information to help us make our assessments, and we believe some of the questions are particularly relevant to the knowledge and skills we seek to develop. (Westinghouse Training Services)

It is true that reading with comprehension is difficult to define, but we do know that children come to the reading task with a great deal of knowledge about the world. It is our job to give them the tools and the confidence to translate that knowledge into contexts which are important to them. In the words of the Chinese proverb:

> If you give a man a fish, you feed him for a day.
> If you teach him *how* to fish, you feed him for a lifetime.

References

BRUNER, J. S. (1966) *Studies in Cognitive Growth* (New York: Wiley).

DAVIDSON, J. (1982) 'The Group Mapping Activity for instruction in reading and thinking', *Journal of Reading*, vol. 26. pp. 52–6.

GRAHAM, A. *et al.* (1980) 'Representing for understanding', *Mathematics across the Curriculum*, Unit 13 (Milton Keynes: The Open University Press).

LUNZER, E. and GARDNER, K. (1979) *The Effective Use of Reading* (London: Heinemann).

LUNZER, E. and GARDNER, K. (1984) *Learning from the Written Word* (Edinburgh: Oliver & Boyd).

MERRITT, J. *et al.* (1977) 'Developing independence in reading', *Reading Development*, Units 5 & 6 (Milton Keynes: The Open University Press).

SHELDON, S. A. (1982) *A Study of Techniques for Teaching and Testing Reading Comprehension* (Unpub. M.Phil. thesis, Open University).

SHELDON, S. A. (1984) 'Comparison of two methods for teaching reading comprehension', *Journal of Research in Reading*, vol. 7, no. 1 pp. 41–52.

STRANG, R. (1968) 'Secondary school reading and thinking', *Reading Teacher*, vol. 21, p. 573.

WILBY, P. (1978) *The Sunday Times*, February.

Chapter 11

The Secondary Student's Approach to Expository Text Processing

Christian Gerhard and Laura Smith

Paragraphs divide text into groups of ideas and form the building materials of text. Students need to apply basic information-processing strategies to them, whether they are reading or writing. Meaning has to be created by finding or expressing the paragraph's main significance and supporting information. Secondary students have to process expository text rather than stories for school tasks, yet many do not know how to do it. Classroom teachers need a practical way of evaluating the ability of students to process groups of ideas which also provides guidance for instruction. This study of 450 paragraphs written by students aged twelve to seventeen, based on four-word categories, is preliminary to a series of studies devoted to filling this need.

Secondary teachers know when their students are unable to do the reading and writing tasks demanded of them, but they may not understand that there can be underlying cause: an ignorance of how ideas are grouped in text.

Regardless of the subject-matter being taught, ideas are grouped by categories, classes, or sets and hierarchies of these. For science and mathematics teachers, the instructional significance of this is obvious, but that is not so for language and history teachers, for example. They are themselves familiar with hierarchies of ideas and it is hard to realise that students may not even see ideas as belonging in groups, but try to deal with them one by one. Neither comprehension nor memory can operate without an understanding of underlying relationships. The most basic of these is the category, or superordinate/subordinate relationship.

Human beings are born with the ability to select the information they attend to, at least up to a point, and the ability to group and code the information in memory. Without this, the brain would be swamped with random sensory impressions and no one would be able to learn from experience or predict likely occurrences. Students, therefore, do have the basic competence of grouping and coding experience, although they are largely unaware of it. In order for the skill to be useful for school tasks, it needs to be understood, consciously applied, and practised on the different kinds of information to be processed.

Processing a paragraph, whether during reading or writing activities, means to find or express a main idea and understand the logical ordering of subordinate points. In other words, in a large proportion of paragraphs to be found in secondary instruction, it means finding the category label and the items whose common attributes have been expressed by the label. The topic sentence is the elaborated equivalent of the category label. In other instances, the reader or writer must infer, or create the possibility of inferring, the generalisation. This too can be done with reference to the category organisation by listing the items and looking for the common attributes. The organisation of many paragraphs, then, has much in common with category structure.

Two additional points need to be made before describing a study of written paragraphs based on categories. The first is that students in secondary classes may not yet have reached the necessary degree of maturity or have accumulated enough concepts to deal with abstract material. The second is that many of the present testing programmes in secondary schools do not have much practical value for teachers and that there is a real need for some form of evaluation, especially of student ability to understand the organisation of ideas in different subject areas.

While Vygotsky, Piaget and Bruner have differences of opinion about other aspects of development, it is accepted that students in the secondary years progress from reliance on the concrete world of actual experience towards a universe of abstract ideas expressed symbolically. A number of studies, such as A. E. Lawson's (Lawson, 1973; Lawson and Blake,

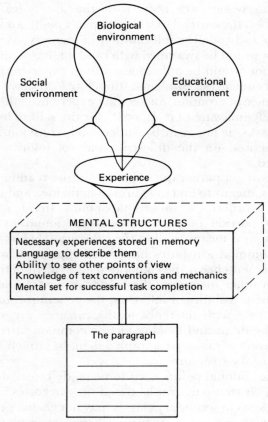

FIGURE 11.1   *Factors affecting paragraph writing*

1976; and Lawson and Wollman, 1976), indicate that even in the final school years many students have not reached a stage of abstract, formal thinking. So Martorano (1974) reviewed a number of studies of adults showing that even among that population this stage has often not been reached. Therefore, a number of tasks demanded of students cannot be successfully completed without a programme of assistance.

Progress is aided or impeded by social, educational and emotional factors which determine not only the way of thinking, but also the intentions, goals or mind sets of students. Language plays an ever-increasing role in all subject areas, including mathematics. Even the creation of one brief paragraph requires an astonishing co-ordination of skills and background information. Recent models, such as J. R. Hayes and L. S. Flowers' (1980) or M. Martlew's (1983), are useful approaches to understanding the complexity of the writing process. Figure 11.1 is the authors' own view of factors affecting the writing of a structured paragraph.

The question inevitably arises whether it is not too late to help students with basic information-processing of abstract materials once they are in upper secondary classes. There is some evidence, such as the work of H. J. Klausmeier and P. S. Allen (1978), that portions of secondary populations are unlikely to progress beyond dealing with the concrete world. On the other hand, the work of H. Taba (1965), R. Feuerstein (1980) and followers of Pascual-Leone such as M. Scardamalia (1977), among many others, seems to indicate that a consistent training programme can be successful, especially for those who have been kept in ignorance of systematic ways of thinking.

The second point mentioned was that present testing programmes on the secondary level are not of great practical value to the classroom teacher, especially if an evaluation of the ability to organise ideas in language, or understand such an organisation, is needed. This study and the projected future studies are an attempt to begin filling this gap.

Description of the study

The study was based on a structured paragraph test developed some years ago by Christian Gerhard as a means of obtaining at least partial information about student thinking and language level. Students are asked to choose one of three groups of four words each to write about. Each group represents a category, the subjects being vehicles, shelter and emotions. The student is asked to select the word which could be a heading for the other three and use that word as a basis for the first sentence of a paragraph. The other three words are then to be used as a basis for three more sentences to complete the paragraph. For example, a word list such as:

> monkey
> dog
> mammals
> whale

would call for a topic sentence based on mammals, followed by a sentence on each of the specific animals.

The population for the study was a private suburban school near Washington, DC. The sample was the entire school divided into six class levels: 7th grade to 12th grade in US terms (students of approximately twelve to seventeen years of age). There were 450 students; the smallest number of any one level was the top class, with 60 students and the lowest class was the largest, with 86 students.

The students wrote the paragraphs in normal English lessons as a preliminary to a possible remedial programme. The instructions were given both orally and in writing. Scoring was done by two graduate assistants who did not know each other, one male, one female, one black and one white. Their instructions were given in writing without special training time in order to simulate the scoring of classroom teachers without training. The scoring was as follows:

> Choice of the correct superordinate word (scoring of either 0 or 5)   5
>
> Writing of an appropriate topic sentence in terms of generalising about the three items (scoring 0 or 2)   2
>
> Use of logical order, a number of different orders being acceptable   1
>
> Writing so that the paragraph makes sense, even if it follows a pattern other than that called for   1
>
> Writing on a level of maturity which could be expected at a given age   1
>
> Total $\underline{\underline{10}}$

The reliability of the two scorers was 0.75.

In addition to the above simple scoring system, the

investigators also noted whether students wrote a narrative rather than expository paragraph, used the first person, and used at least one complex sentence. Numbers of boys and girls writing about each of the three subjects on each class level and their success at writing a structured paragraph was also noted.

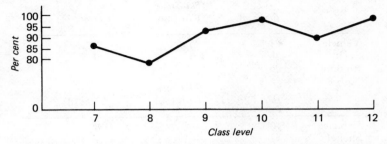

FIGURE 11.2   *Percentage on each class level choosing the superordinate word correctly*

Figure 11.2 shows the percentage of students on each class level who chose the correct superordinate word. Figure 11.3 sorts the three subjects written on by boys and girls by class level and the percentage of those who chose the correct superordinate word. Figure 11.4 shows the percentage of students on each level who wrote a narrative rather than an expository paragraph and those who used the first person. Figure 11.5 summarises the percentage on each grade level who wrote at least one complex sentence and the relationship of this to choice of the correct superordinate word.

Discussion of the study

This study has certain limitations which must be dealt with at the outset. It is descriptive and exploratory, the population of suburban middle-class students prevents any generalisation to secondary students as a whole, there is no random sampling, and clearly the paragraph test is not a good indicator of the capacity of students to write a sophisticated paragraph or longer passages. Results may also be distorted because of the inability of students to follow directions rather than their

	Boys (n = 46)	7th grade Girls (n = 40)	Total (n = 86)
Vehicles	13	11	12
Shelter	31	9	16
Emotions	—	—	—

	Boys (38)	8th Grade Girls (36)	Total (74)
Vehicles	21	25	23
Shelter	36	6	20
Emotions	25	—	14

	Boys (49)	9th Grade Girls (36)	Total (85)
Vehicles	10	—	8
Shelter	7	—	4
Emotions	—	10	9

	Boys (44)	10th Grade Girls (32)	Total (76)
Vehicles	6	11	7
Shelter	—	—	—
Emotions	—	—	—

	Boys (38)	11th Grade Girls (31)	Total (69)
Vehicles	18	13	17
Shelter	—	22	10
Emotions	—	7	6

	Boys (38)	12th Grade Girls (22)	Total (60)
Vehicles	—	—	—
Shelter	—	—	—
Emotions	14	—	7

FIGURE 11.3 *Percentage of girls and boys on each grade level who chose an incorrect superordinate word sorted by the category they chose to write on*

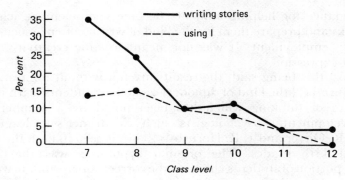

Note: The use of 'I' changed in the 10th class level to being predominantly included in 'I think', 'I believe' type of constructions.

FIGURE 11.4 *Percentage on each class level writing story paragraphs and using 'I' (first person)*

Grade level	Per cent writing complex sentences	Per cent choosing correct superordinate word
7th	65	84
8th	45	69
9th	42	94
10th	75	93
11th	68	87
12th	43	95

FIGURE 11.5 *Percentage of students writing complex sentences compared to choosing the correct superordinate word by grade level*

inability to write a paragraph. The authors have had opportunities to observe that this is the case in other populations. Future studies include an ethnographic follow-up with extensive interviews.

There is also a danger in stressing the writing of structure expository paragraphs. J. Britton and his colleagues (1975) have shown how limiting writing only for teacher evaluation can be. Especially in adolescence, students need opportunities for working through their personal experiences. The paragraph test was developed in the hopes that it would offer some guidance for helping students become competent at school tasks and prepare them for the kind of writing often associated with employment. It was not meant to stifle creativity and self-expression.

All this being said, the results are not without interest. In Figure 11.2 the kind of dip or regression as students learn new ways of thinking which has been noted by a number of developmental psychologists such as Bruner's colleagues, R. R. Oliver and J. R. Hornsby (1966), is seen in both the 8th and 11th grades. The original hypothesis was that the proportion of students choosing the correct superordinate word in each word group would increase from the youngest to the oldest class. This was substantiated if the classes are grouped by the three youngest and the three oldest. The difference was significant at the $p<.05$ level. However, there was not a linear progression.

In line with a history of reports that girls are more competent with language than boys up to about the age of sixteen, the hypothesis was made that girls would choose the correct superordinate word more often than boys. This did not prove to be the case. However, a look at Figure 11.3 reveals a complex relationship between sex, age and subject chosen as they affect correct choice. This result agrees with a number of studies which indicate that there is no monolithic writing ability, even for one individual. The type of task, the writer's perception of the audience, individual experience and schooling, familiarity with literature, and many other variables affect results.

It was hypothesised that there would be a significantly larger proportion of students in the two youngest classes writing narrative paragraphs and using the first person than in the older four classes. The hypothesis was based both on developmental grounds and the effect of schooling. The difference between the two groups, illustrated in Figure 11.4, was highly significant at the $p<.001$ level for writing narrative paragraphs and significant at the $p<.05$ level for use of the first person. It should be noted that the use of the first person changed in the third class and above to forms such as 'I believe' or 'I think' rather than a personal narrative use such as 'I saw' or 'I did'.

Figure 11.5 is offered to show how much work remains to be

done in this area. The way in which relationships are expressed is certainly relevant to a study of how students organise groups of ideas in language. However, detailed analysis must wait. A preliminary examination indicated that students in the two oldest classes used more sophisticated vocabulary and appropriate compound sentences than did the younger students, often making complex sentences unnecessary. It was also interesting to note that in the 4th and 5th oldest classes, students sometimes used a higher level of superordination than the one provided; for example, writing about *transportation* rather than *vehicles*. Clearly, they understood which word was superordinate, but overshot the mark.

In summary, results substantiate models showing writing as a highly complex process, even though the study was based on simple, short paragraphs only. There do also appear to be certain developmental trends, especially in regard to the use of expository rather than narrative form, which are probably affected by both development and schooling.

Future plans

A teacher of reading will want to understand the relationship between ability to write a paragraph and ability to understand the organisation of ideas when reading. One study, by W. P. Lazdowski (1976), predicted reading grade levels accurately within one grade from writing samples taken from a range of ages. There has also been substantial work done on the relationship between reading and writing, such as that by W. Kintsch and T. A. Van Dijk (1978), R. J. Tierney and D. P. Pearson (1983), and S. Stotsky (1983).

It seems only logical to assume that certain aspects of paragraph *writing* might indicate possible strengths or weaknesses in *reading* paragraphs. A lack of understanding of paragraph form, choice of a subordinate word as the main topic, lack of logical order, difficulty in expressing relationships, or use of limited vocabulary might well indicate related problems in reading. Further research is necessary to establish predictable relationships.

Studies looking at correlations between written paragraphs

and standardised reading and intelligence tests are under way and await the accumulation of a sufficient number of samples. At one university reading centre the paragraph test is included with each test battery administered. This centre also uses the test as an indicator of the type of tutoring called for. An extensive checksheet for use with individuals has been found practical and could be used by classroom teachers interested in more than a quick scoring.

The co-operation of many people will be necessary to accumulate large numbers of paragraphs from different populations. Results may show that populations differ as to their place on a continuum of development, which would in turn call for different kinds of instruction.

Informal attempts to create bridges for students between the categorising they do in daily life and that which they need to do to be successful in secondary classes have been going on for some years (Gerhard, 1975). More recently, twenty teachers from one school were trained to use the process of categorising to help their students think more systematically. The training included developing subject-matter categories for writing-to-learn activities. Recent research has shown this, as well as carefully planned reading, to be an effective tool (Bereiter, 1980; Emig, 1977; Fulwiler, 1982; Newell, 1984; and Shanklin, 1982). In the coming year the progress of students in the classes of the trained teachers will be monitored through paragraph writing.

All of this is preliminary to setting up experimental studies using analysis of paragraphs written by students as a dependent variable in training programmes. This should be done in a variety of classes. One study (Gerhard, 1983) seems to indicate that language and history teachers need some assistance in working with the categorising process to improve comprehension, recall and written expression.

The authors wish to thank Marilyn Binkley, presently of The National Institute of Education, Washington, DC, for assistance in obtaining the paragraph samples.

References

BEREITER, C. (1980) 'Development in writing', in L. W. Gregg and E. R. Sternberg, *Cognitive Processes in Writing* (Hillsdale, New Jersey, Erlbaum), pp. 73–93.

BRITTON, J., BURGESS, T. *et al.* (1975) *The Development of Writing Abilities (11–18)* (London: Macmillan).

FEUERSTEIN, R. (1980) *Instrumental Enrichment: An Intervention Program for Cognitive Modifiability* (Baltimore, Maryland: University Park).

FULWILER, T. (1982) 'The personal connection: Journal writing across the curriculum', in T. Fulwiler and A. Young (eds) *Language Connections: Writing and Reading Across the Curriculum* (Urbana, Illinois: The National Council of Teachers of English).

GERHARD, C. (1975) *Making Sense: Reading Comprehension Improved Through Categorizing* (Newark, Delaware: International Reading Association).

GERHARD, C. (1983) 'Teacher knowledge about selected aspects of categorizing and their use in the instruction of sixth, seventh, and eighth grade students' (Unpublished dissertation, George Washington University).

HAYES, J. R. and FLOWER, L. S. (1980) 'Identifying the organization of writing processes', in L. W. Gregg and E. R. Sternberg (eds) *Cognitive Processes in Writing* (Hillsdale, New Jersey: Erlbaum), pp. 3–30.

KINTSCH, W. and VAN DIJK, T. A. (1978) 'Toward a model of text comprehension and production', *Psychological Review*, no. 85, pp. 363–76.

KLAUSMEIER, H. J. and ALLEN, P. S. (1978) *Cognitive Development of Children and Youth: A Longitudinal Study* (New York: Academic Press).

LAWSON, A. E. (1973) 'Relationships between concrete and formal-operational science subject matter and the intellectual level of the learner' (Unpublished dissertation, University of Oklahoma).

LAWSON and BLAKE, A. J. D. (1976) 'Concrete and formal thinking abilities in high school biology students as measured by three separate instruments', *Journal of Research in Science Teaching*, no. 13, pp. 227–35.

LAWSON and WOLLMAN, W. (1976) 'Encouraging the transition from concrete to formal cognitive functioning – An Experiment', *Journal of Research in Science Teaching*, no. 13, pp. 413–30.

LAZDOWSKI, W. P. (1976) 'Determining reading grade levels from analysis of written compositions' (Unpublished dissertation, University of New Mexico).

MARTORANO, S. (1974) 'The development of formal operational thought' (Unpublished dissertation, Rutgers University).

MARTLEW, M. (1983) 'Problems and difficulties; Cognitive and communicative aspects of writing', in M. Martlew (ed.) *The Psychology of Written Language* (New York: John Wiley), pp. 295–333.

NEWELL, G. E. (1984) 'Learning from writing in two content areas: A case study/protocol analysis', *Research in the Teaching of English*, no. 18, pp. 265–87.

OLVER, R. R. and HORNSBY, J. R. (1966) 'On equivalence', in J. S. Bruner, R. R.

Olver and F. M. Greenfield (eds) *Studies in Cognitive Growth* (New York: John Wiley).

SCARDAMALIA, M. (1977) 'Information processing capacity and the problem of horizontal decalage: A demonstration using combinatorial reasoning tasks', *Child Development*, no. 48, pp. 28–37.

SHANKLIN, N. (1982) 'Relating reading to writing: Developing a transactional theory of the writing process' (Unpublished dissertation, University of Indiana).

STOTSKY, S. (1983) 'Research of reading/writing relationships: A synthesis and suggested directions' *Language Arts*, no. 60, pp. 627–43.

TABA, H. (1965) 'The teaching of thinking', *Elementary English*, no. 42, pp. 534–42.

TIERNEY, R. J. and PEARSON, D. P. (1983) 'Toward a composing model of reading', *Language Arts*, no. 60, pp. 568–80.

Chapter 12

Appraising Phonic Resources

Joyce Morris

Collectively, educational publishers have provided plenty of phonic resources from which teachers of English reading and spelling may choose. On the whole, they have also improved the 'surface' characteristics of these resources in terms of attractiveness, durability and so on. But, with notable exceptions, critical appraisal reveals that what they have generally failed to do is ensure that each resource is based on sound linguistic knowledge of the nature of English in spoken and written form.

The need for improvement

In recent years, the writer has drawn attention to the need for educational publishers to rectify this unsatisfactory situation. Several have responded confidentially in writing, especially to an article in *Reading* (Morris, 1984). Clearly they would like to make amends but are handicapped by the lack of authors who have the necessary linguistic knowledge coupled with practical experience of using phonic resources in the classroom. In oral discussion, other publishers have pointed out that some of the phonic resources which, in one way or another, are unsound from a linguistic standpoint are very successful commercially. Therefore, in these hard times for educational publishing, it would be foolhardy to cease reprinting them. Moreover, it must be remembered that, at present, they provide essential revenue to support the publication of materials for other important curriculum areas.

In the circumstances, it would seem that a marked improvement will only come about when all teachers of initial literacy have the time and *explicit* linguistic knowledge to look below the surface characteristics of phonic resources and critically appraise them in terms of their linguistic content. Unfortunately, the demands on practising teachers are such that finding time to do this thoroughly will always be very difficult, and it is unlikely that a high proportion will achieve the necessary *explicit* knowledge unless the need for applied linguistics in teacher education is not only widely recognised but catered for in pre-servce and in-service courses.

At present there are hopeful signs in, for example, the formation of the 'UKRA Special Interest Group on Linguistics in Teacher Education' during the Association's 22nd annual conference at Reading University. Thanks to the President, delegates also had opportunities not only to debate the motion, 'Phonics is Essential to Provision for Literacy', but also to participate in a workshop on the appraisal of phonic resources with 'Phonics 44' as the linguistics-informed model.

Introduction to linguistics-informed appraisal

The three workshop sessions were conducted by the writer and Jeanne Nickson, Resources Officer at the Language and Reading Centre of the Roehampton Institute of Higher Education, located in Digby Stuart College. She mounted a support display of published materials which illustrate the main strengths and weaknesses of phonic resources available to British teachers. It included items generously donated by educational publishers for critical appraisal by workshop participants and for subsequent use in the Digby Stuart Centre.

At the outset, attention was drawn to the abundance of phonic resources as catalogued by B. Root (1982) and by D. Herbert and G. Davies-Jones (1984). Discussion followed on the varieties of Standard English which naturally affect the content of such resources because they are concerned with relationships between speech sounds (phonemes) and the graphic symbols (graphemes) of traditional orthography. Here particular attention was paid to differences in the number of vowel sounds in, for instance, North American English and Southern English English. Also highlighted were the differential effects of rhotic accents which actually pronounce 'r' corresponding to orthographic 'r' in words like *far* and *farm*

APPRAISAL FORM FOR PHONIC RESOURCES

(using Morris 'Phonics 44' as the linguistics-informed model)

Appraisal by ....
Name, author, publisher and date of the phonic resource

....

Country of origin (for rhotic/non-rhotic differences) ....

A. CLASSIFICATION (Please tick on the appropriate line)

1. Type   ......   complete scheme independent of basal reading/language scheme
          ......   complete scheme ancillary to basal reading/language scheme
          ......   complete scheme incorporated in books of basal scheme
          ......   individual items with no recommended sequence
          ......   a single item

2. Form .../...   game/games
         .../...   teaching aid/aids
         .../...   tape/tapes and software
         .../...   phonic workbooks/SDM's
       .../.../... phonic tests diagnostic/achievement/both
          ......   phonic workshop
          ......   books for children only
          ......   books for teachers only
          ......   books for children and their teachers

3. Phonic Approach   .../... ...   analytic/synthetic
                     .../.../...   for reading/spelling/both

B. IS THE PHONIC RESOURCE LINGUISTICS-INFORMED?

(Please write Yes or No before each statement)

1.   ......   The terms 'phonic' and 'phonetic' are correctly used.
2a.   ......   Consonant *sounds* and consonant *letters* are clearly distinguished.
 b.   ......   Vowel *sounds* and vowel *letters* are clearly distinguished.
3a.   ......   The number of consonant *sounds* referred to is 24.
 b.   ......   The 'redundancy' of consonant *letters* c, q, x is understood.
 c.   ......   The equivalence of *ck* and 'twin' consonant letters e.g., *ff* is recognised.
 d.   ......   The 6 consonant sounds represented by digraphs *sh*, *ch*, *th*, and other letter combinations are presented as conforming to the alphabetic principle but with distinctive characteristics.
 e.   ......   A clear distinction is made between consonant digraphs and so-called consonant 'blends' such as *cl* and *scr*.
4a.   ......   The number of vowel *sounds* referred to is 20 (non-rhotic RP).
 b.   ......   A clear distinction is made between vowel digraphs such as *ai* and vowel trigraphs such as *air*.
5.   ......   The 'Schwa' or weak stress vowel represented, for example, by *er*, and *ar*, as in caterpillar is distinguished from *er* and *ar* representing the vowel phonemes in fern and farm respectively.
6a.   ......   Recognition is given to differences between visual and sound patterns in words when using rhymes in an 'analytic' approach.
 b.   ......   Recognition is given to orthographic structure in the provision of examples for a 'synthetic' phonic approach e.g., the *ba* sequence (bad, bag, ban) not (bake, bail, bar, bare).
7.   ......   Words described as 'irregular' or 'divergent' indicate knowledge of the nature of English orthography in that they include words such as 'one' and 'many' but not, for example, some of the *ho* sequence i.e., hope, hoot, hook, horse, house, hoist.
8.   ......   The format of the resource accords with its educational aim e.g., a marker or 'magic' *e* game is not presented on the illustration of an 'engine'.

FIGURE 12.1   *Appraisal form for phonic resources*

and non-rhotic accents which do not. Hence the educational significance of teachers noting first the country from which a particular phonic resource originates.

The first workshop session was then devoted to a slide-accompanied explanation of 'Phonics 44' and to the rationale behind the appraisal form for phonic resources shown in Figure 12.1. As will be seen, Part A is concerned with classifying the type, form and phonic approach of a particular resource based on the classification devised by Root (1982), whereas Part B is a series of statements designed by the writer to answer the fundamentally important question of whether a particular resource is 'linguistics-informed'. Accordingly, a completely affirmative answer would require the word 'Yes' to be written beside each of the fifteen statements arranged in eight categories. Naturally also, the more 'No' statements, the less sound the phonic resource from a linguistic standpoint.

Discussion of the results

The participants spent the second workshop session studying a phonic resource of their choice from the display and then recording the results on the appraisal form provided. Some, despite being experienced teachers, confessed to finding the exercise difficult, especially in the time allotted. But everyone appeared to find it stimulating, thought-provoking and of practical use.

One participant is an editor for a leading publisher, and she selected for her appraisal a phonic resource which she had doubts about although it is a great and continuing commercial success for her company. Understandably, her completed appraisal form must remain confidential and her anonymity be preserved. However, it is interesting to note that for Part B, 'Yes' was recorded beside only four of the fifteen statements and 'No' beside six of them. As for the rest, three spaces were left, one was considered 'not applicable' and the last was starred with a note explaining that the formats of the accompanying spiritmasters 'diverge from the original educational aim of the scheme'. In short, completing the appraisal form had confirmed doubts about that popular phonic resource and convinced her that, in future, phonic resources submitted for publication by her company should be 'vetted' by a 'real' expert in the phonics field.

Towards the end of the final workshop session, participants came together to discuss their novel experience and to make suggestions as to how the appraisal form might be improved to be of even greater use to teachers. Clearly, what they had discovered had been something of a shock to them and they were keen to see the marked improvement that is generally required in phonic resources. Meanwhile, they suggested that the appraisal form would be improved by the inclusion of a 'not applicable' category for statements in Part B, and by the addition of a final point on the check list, that is, 'Guidance is given to the teacher regarding pronunciation'. Furthermore, they felt that, at the bottom of the form, teachers should be invited to answer the following questions:

(a) Would you use this material, in spite of mistakes, because of its motivation for children?
(b) If you feel that this material cannot be used in its present form, what would you change and how?

Future prospects

With these and other amendments, the above appraisal form will be subjected to further workshop trials with a view to its publication for use in training teachers in the critical evaluation of phonic resources. Clearly, this kind of development is long overdue. In the interests of their pupils, and bearing in mind the economic situation, teachers cannot 'afford' to make wrong choices. It is, therefore, important that, in future, they have adequate training to look below the surface characteristics of classroom materials. It is equally important that any phonic resource advertised as 'new' should be such as to warrant a guarantee of 'soundness' from a linguistic standpoint.

References

HERBERT, D. and DAVIES-JONES, G. (1984) *A Classroom Index of Phonic Resources* (Stafford: NARE Publications).

MORRIS, J. M. (1984) 'Phonics 44 for initial literacy in English', *Reading*, vol. 18, pp. 13–23.

ROOT, B. (1982) *Resources for Teaching Phonics* (Centre for the Teaching of Reading, School of Education, University of Reading).

Part IV

Implications for Classroom Practice (Children's Writing)

Chapter 13

The Productive Process: An Approach to Literacy for Children with Difficulties

Margaret L. Peters and Brigid Smith

Children with learning difficulties need to be helped to move from learned helplessness to autonomy in reading and writing. As a kind of speaking, writing emerges from the dictated story. This is the origin of highly acceptable reading material; for these stories are in the idiom and context of the child writer. Competence in transcription has to be learned, and this only comes from an internalised knowledge of the orthography. The secretarial skills must be taught, and not during the composing, but in advance, and in the sense of knowing the nature of the orthography. Children's understanding of story and story language, emerging through a Language Experience Approach provides that feeling of competence in writing that many children do not know they possess. The value of word-processing is in the separation of composition from transcription. The technique lends itself to this separation and makes drafting and redrafting motivating and effective. Reflection time is an integral part of the word processing activity and this aids the drive towards cognitive clarity in communication.

> **We have known for years the child's first urge is to write and not read and we haven't taken advantage of this fact. We have underestimated the power of the output languages like speaking and writing.**
>
> (Durrell, quoted in Graves, 1978)

This paper looks at ways in which children with difficulties in literacy can be helped to move from dependency and passivity in their learning, towards a positive and active attitude to the task of learning to read and write. When pupils can understand the strategies which make readers and writers effective, then they are able to move from learned helplessness to effective autonomy – a state in which they are in control of their learning and know how to approach and overcome their difficulties.

A shift in emphasis is necessary if pupils are to become confident and competent readers and writers. A shift from dependency, negativity and a sense of working in the dark, to active participation and a learning partnership in which self-correction and the ability to be self-critical are inherent in the process of becoming self-controlled in reading and writing.

Children coming into the comprehensive school unable to read are just as aware of their reading disability as of their inability to write. Repeated and varied pressures have been put upon them to read. Six years of phonics, simple reading books and 'activity work books' have had no effect on their reading. And what they neither want nor need is 'more of the same'.

There has not been the same kind of pressure on their writing. Their teacher was always there to 'give them a word' and to correct their mistakes. She may have written at the end of their bit of writing, 'Mind your spelling' or 'Learn the word "bought"!' – instructions which, even if they could be read would not in any sense help the child. 'Learned helplessness' was perenially effective! The effort of writing something down, however ill-spelt and poorly constructed, is seen to be the end of the pupil's part in the writing process. Correcting mistakes is the job of the teacher.

In recent years the move towards all pupils being taught, where possible, in mainstream classes has radically changed the role of the remedial teacher. It is no longer merely support for pupils with individual needs which is demanded – now the particular skills of the remedial teacher must be shared and made available to all teachers. The expertise and experience of the remedial teacher must help to reshape subject curriculum and methodology so that all pupils can learn in a well-resourced and supported way to be successful and to realise their own potential. The task for the teacher of special needs pupils lies as much in the 'reskilling of the deskilled' amongst teaching colleagues as it does in the preparation of materials and resources to meet the pupil's needs in the mainstream lesson.

The partnership in learning which this necessarily involves is a sharing of expertise and a commitment to starting to teach at the point which the pupil has reached. Learning has to be seen as a continuum and all pupils as being at different points on that continuum. In school and subject curriculum planning the model must be of a spiral rather than a linear curriculum, with pupils 'revisiting' points in the curriculum at different levels as their skills and understanding increase. All subject teachers need to be aware of the strategies and special resources which can support the learning of pupils with special needs.

Teaching pupils the strategies for learning new words and subject vocabulary, how to redraft their writing so that they communicate clearly what they know, how to reach understanding through the mediation of talk and how to read for meaning will give them the necessary skills to cope in the mainstream classroom. The pupil has to have the confidence to take part, to produce writing, to read and to talk – and then to be reflective and self-corrective with the product of these efforts.

In order to make effective learning partnerships with the pupils, they need to start with what they already know – the words they already know how to write and the words they need to know in order to communicate what they want to say. They already have the oral skills to make the bridge between utterance and text (Olson, 1977). The reading and writing which they undertake has to be seen by them to be purposeful, to have an audience and to be part of the mainstream curriculum involving real educational ideas and methodologies. Most importantly, the pupils must feel confident of success.

The productive process of writing, made effective by the confidence derived from an understanding of the orthography and how spelling works; reading which capitalises on oral skills and immediate success for the reader; and the new technology which makes redrafting and editing of writing a pleasurable and motivating activity are three of the ways in which pupils can be helped to move from dependency to autonomy.

So a complete change of demand and of objective is essential, and this change comes about through a two-pronged attack on literacy. This takes the form of capitalising on children's oral language skills in order to provide reading resources, while simultaneously facilitating spelling competence as a tool for the production of quality writing.

The writing process

An understanding of the separation of the process of writing into the role of author and secretary is necessary if pupils are to be helped to produce writing of quality (F. Smith, 1982).

The writer needs to know that he has two roles to play so that anxiety about the technical aspects of writing do not interfere with the impetus to communicate an idea or story. The teacher has to help the writer to see that first time writing is not the end of the process. Sharing with the writer the ways in which competent adults reflect, rehearse and redraft their writing until the sense of it comes clear, and giving writers a code to use in their redrafting (Binns, 1980) allows them to 'take over' the task of clarifying and extending their own writing.

Encouraging the pupil to read a first draft on to tape and then to listen, so that the passage can be punctuated meaningfully, helps writers to take the listening/reflecting role and so to understand the importance of making clear what it is they want to say. The understanding of the way in which punctuation works is a by-product of this activity. In this way concentration on the author role in writing can be considered separately from concern about spelling and handwriting.

Competence in transcription has to be learned, and this only comes from an internalised knowledge of the orthography. These secretarial skills are dependent on awareness of the nature of the English orthography, the awareness that it is systematic (Peters, 1985). Such knowledge is essential to the child, but even more to the teacher. The teacher must be aware that 'spelling is a kind of grammar for letter sequences that generates permissible combinations without regard to sound' (Gibson and Levin, 1975). In other words, only some letters can follow other letters, and it is not the sound of the word that tells us what letters can follow other letters, but the look of the letter sequence, whether or not it is a likely sequence or letter string, that is to say, whether it 'could happen'. This is the basis of autonomy in spelling, when a child can look at a word and see that it 'couldn't happen'. Such autonomy depends on the growing knowledge of possible and probable letter strings provided by the teacher, who has not only a model of the orthography but knows what the model looks like.

Teachers are pedantic in their approach to spelling. They ask children to look through their work and underline what words *they* think are wrong. But teachers are interested, not in the words the pupils recognise to be wrong but those they do *not* know are wrong, for it is here that there is evidence of the pupils' lack of knowledge of the spelling system. So, if a child writes 'bouthe' for 'bought', the letter string 'ought' needs teaching, as in 'cough, dough, enough,' etc. – words which look the same even though they do not sound the same. It is not the sound but the look of the word that matters in spelling. Again, a teacher may teach the letter string 'app', which a child can write a number of times. Then the teacher says 'Put *that* in front and *that* at the end' pointing while saying '*that*' to letters or letter strings to add. (The teacher does not say the name or sound of the letter, for the child has to look.) Children find themselves writing words that might have seemed difficult, and this brings a kind of status knowledge, for they find they can not only spell 'apple' and 'happy', but also 'disappoint', 'disappear', 'applause', and, as one school leaver found to his satisfaction, 'applications' and 'appointment'.

This teaching of serial probability, which is what we are sensitising children to in the practice of letter strings, can occur in a group with swift blackboard writing and rubbing out. It can occur for a short time at the beginning of a group writing session, or introduce specialist words in different disciplines across the curriculum.

The important thing is to facilitate spelling, to give children confidence to write a word without needing to ask the teacher how to spell it, knowing that at some later stage of redrafting a kindly hand will direct the child to 'what it is like' – for example, 'notice' . . . 'Oh, it's got "ice" in it like "police" and "office" . . .'. Generalisation of letter strings is taking place, and taking place in a very low key.

Spelling and other secretarial skills should not be the first objective in redrafting. Whether in discussing with the teacher an early handwritten or word-processed draft, the conference between the teacher and child should not be concerned with spelling but the aim should be to increase cognitive clarity. When children are really satisfied with what they have written, then they can go through the final draft and underline the spellings they know are incorrect. Then, and only then, will the teacher help, possibly by writing the correct version at the side. The child, trained so as not merely to copy, will learn the spelling as he writes it from memory.

A way into reading

Failed and failing readers often see reading as something 'out there' – a key or code which they cannot 'get'. We know that in oral skills such pupils are able to negotiate for meaning, to make themselves understood – talk is an interactive, predictive, self-correcting, meaning-making activity. All these skills are necessary for reading, too. The problem with reading is knowing, in the triumvirate of reader, author and text, where the meaning lies (Chapman, 1981). Talk has shared meanings, is interpretative and explicit – text is remote, unsupported and does not give us clues as it proceeds (Olson, 1977). For pupils whose knowledge of literacy is limited the bridging of this gap between the language that children bring to school with them and the language of school texts is crucial. We need texts for failing readers which are meaningful, predictable, psychologically compatible, have the status of a 'real' book and that can be read successfully first time round.

We need to capitalise on children's oral skills and the need to make a narrative, to tell 'the story that must be told' (Meek, 1980). When children dictate their own reading books these criteria are met and the texts which are created are real texts. The bridge can be the '. . . common bridge for a child of any race and of more moment than any other: the bridge from the inner world outward' (Ashton-Warner, 1963).

The practicalities of using a language experience approach

A brief description of using this method with eleven-year-old non-readers in a comprehensive school may indicate practical ways in which such an approach to reading can be organised. Volunteer helpers are paired with pupils with poor reading skills. In a weekly session of one hour, pupils dictate a chapter of their story. This story is typed into a printed text for them. Using a method devised by T. Glynn (1980) to train parents to listen to reading, the volunteers have been able to respond confidently and consistently to the pupils' reading. There are many language activities which arise during the course of the sessions and the importance of the talk between the volunteer and the reader/writer is central to the whole process. Initial research into this area would seem to indicate that as readers become more confident and as they achieve success in their reading they also become more self-corrective in their reading and more adventurous and complex in their use of language in the story. Further developments may show that the reflecting/ editing role in writing is mirrored in the dictating/reading/ reflecting which occurs in this language experience approach to reading.

The generalisation from reading dictated text to text written by someone else may be seen in the following example of an eleven-year-old. Dean came to secondary school from a special school. He was a very poor and anxious reader and was not able to tolerate the possibility of making mistakes. His resistance to reading books and reading material was considerable and his anxiety created a barrier between him and the teacher trying to teach him to read. In his new school no other reading was done with him besides his own dictated texts. He dictated a lively and interesting story about his mum winning at bingo and the family all going to Australia on a cruise. It was necessary to research books, write to Australia House for information and use maps in order to get the story background right. Dean read his book with enthusiasm and confidence and, as the story progressed, he 'wrote in' characters from the school – the teacher, the welfare assistant and finally the headmaster – who, in the story, had aspirations to being a surfer. The passage about surfing proved difficult for Dean to dictate as his knowledge of surfing was not very great. The scribe offered to write a passage in. Realising that this was a risk – that the confidence and security with which Dean approached his reading of his own words could be jeopardised by a failure at this point it was with considerable trepidation that the following passage was written in for Dean:

> Dean dictated:
>> One day Mr Street bought a surfing board.
>> He did not know nothing about surfing.
>> He went out to the sea.
> The teacher then added for him:
>> Dean said he would show him.
>> Dean got a board and paddled far out into the waves.
>> The waves were even bigger now.
>> An enormous wave rose up high into the air.
>> Dean stood up on the board.
>> He felt the shudder of the water running under the board.
>> He stood up and raised his arms.
>> With a great rush the wave went high into the air.
>> Dean stood up high above the water and the surf board
>>   rose up on the wave,
>> Dean was thirty feet above the water.
>> Then the wave broke.
>> The surf was thundering into the shore. Dean came in on
>>   his board.
>> Everyone on the beach cheered and clapped.
>> Dean sat down on the beach.
>> 'That's how its done!' he said.

Dean read the whole passage without hesitation, passing from his own dictated text to text written for him without faltering. He was reading unknown, unsupported text with fluency and intention to make sense of what it said. The fact that he was the competent, superior and achieving hero of the text was no doubt of significance in his performance! The fact that he had a ready audience in the headmaster, who listened with pleasure and approval to Dean's reading and accepted his own learner role in the story was also no doubt important in the development of Dean's reading competence and confidence.

In another instance Robert's volunteer scribe interspersed technical book language, taken from a car manual, into Robert's story about his father's car:

> My Dad's got two cars; a Range Rover and an Avenger – that's me mum's. It's orange.
> The Talbot Avenger is a two-door or four-door saloon or estate with 1.3 or 1.6 litre engine.
> First introduced over ten years ago but there are still plenty on the road.

Robert too read this confidently. Generalisation can be helped by such means. Success and practice of reading skills also give pupils the confidence to view themselves as readers and so to approach the reading of other texts with more confidence.

The process of learning to be a reader/writer may be a crucial element in learning to read. It allows children to have an insight into the process of both reading and writing. They are taking a position which straddles both roles. In literary criticism this is a vital position analogous to Roland Barthes' (1976) 'inter-text', the seam of the text in which meaning is exchanged. It is this understanding that can help children not only to discover reading as a meaningful and positive activity but also allow them the experience which will enable them, as writers, to take a reader/reflector role in order to be self-corrective and to redraft their writing to make it clearer.

Using the word-processor to help pupils to think about writing

The use of the word-processor allows a clear distinction to be made between the composing and the transcribing process. The word-processor helps children to reflect on their writing, to redraft not just the surface structure, improving the secretarial skills, but encouraging the cognitive skills of drafting and redrafting at deep structure level to take place. The children, in rehearsing to themselves what they have written, take on the role of reader/reflector.

The technical processes involved in using the processor allow pupils the time and space to reflect and provide the motivation to redraft work. The possibility, at the end, of producing a neatly printed piece of work is a powerful goal for poor writers. The necessity of waiting for a turn at the processor can aid the writing process, persuading pupils to plan their work so as not to waste time when they get their turn. The production of a print-out allows them to take away the story and to work on it, adding, changing and clarifying. When they return to redraft their work it is immediately accessible from disk and they can start at the point of redraft. Many children will work through several written drafts before reaching a final print-out. Richard Binns (1980) suggests a code for redrafting which has been found to give children real autonomy in their writing.

The process of writing, reading, reflecting, using the code to find spelling difficulties and to decide where changes and expansions need to be made puts the responsibility for change and communication on to the pupil. (Fuller details of using the word-processor can be found in B. M. Smith, 1985.) Tony (aged thirteen) referred to his work as 'extending it until it is perfect' at a time when he was on a fourth or fifth draft of his story.

The word-processor allows pupils and teachers to work in partnership, producing work where quality, not quantity, is of paramount importance. The control lies with the pupil – both over the machine and over the redrafting of the writing. By experiencing this power and autonomy children can be changed from passive or hostile non-participants in reading and writing into enthusiastic practitioners. They are not changed by practising irrelevant or repetitious exercises but rather by the experience of becoming controllers of their own learning and by the powerful experience of standing at the centre of the reading and writing process.

References

ASHTON-WARNER, S. (1963) *Teacher* (London: Secker & Warburg).
BARTHES, R. (1976) *The Pleasure of the Text* (London: Jonathan Cape).
BINNS, R. (1980) 'A technique for developing written language', in *Reading and Writing for the Child with Difficulties*, M. M. Clark and T. Glynn (eds), Educational Review Occasional Publication no. 8 (University of Birmingham).

CHAPMAN, L. J. (1981) 'The Reader and the Text,' Presidential address in *The Reader and the Text*, L. J. Chapman (ed.) (London: Heinemann Educational).

GIBSON, E. J. and LEVIN, H. (1975) *The Psychology of Reading* (Harvard, Mass.: MIT Press).

GLYNN, T. (1980) 'Parent-Child Interaction in Remedial Reading at Home', *Reading and Writing for the Child with Difficulties* M. Clark and T. Glynn (eds), Educational Review Occasional Publication no. 8 (University of Birmingham).

GRAVES, D. H. (1978) *Balance the BASICS*, paper on research about learning (Ford Foundation).

MEEK, M. (1980) Prolegomena for a Study of Children's Literature', *Approaches to Research in Children's Literature* M. Benton, (ed.) (Department of Education University of Southampton).

OLSON, D. R. (1977) 'From Utterance to Text: the Bias of Language in Speech and Writing', *Harvard Educational Review* vol. 47, no. 3, pp. 257–81.

PETERS, M. L. (1985) *Spelling Caught or Taught: A New Look* (London: Routledge & Kegan Paul).

SMITH, B. M. (1985) 'Using the word-processor to help children to think about writing', *Micro-Explorations* no. 2 F. Potter and D. Wray (eds) (Ormskirk: UKRA).

SMITH, F. (1982) *Writing and the Writer* (London: Heinemann).

Chapter 14

Reading Resources and Children's Writing

Roger Beard

For some years now, a succession of reports have indicated that we need to extend the range of the writing which children do in schools. This paper will indicate how this range may be supported and extended by a more sensitive use of resources which children read and have read to them. The main focus of the paper will be on the ways in which the quality of textual organisation of these resources can be better used in helping primary and middle school children fulfil a variety of aims in writing.

The past decade has seen a burgeoning of observational research in schools which has made us more aware of general strengths and weaknesses in the organisation and curriculum of schools. It is important to note that this research has identified many creditable features of current practice, but here I will concentrate on some aspects where weaknesses have been detected. The survey of eighty first schools by Her Majesty's Inspectors (DES, 1982) reports that in many schools there was an excessive and purposeless use of English textbook exercises and commercially produced assignment cards, so that some children had too little time for personal writing.

The study by N. Bennett *et al.* (1984) of sixteen able teachers of six- and seven-year-olds, reports that in most classes there was a lack of sequence, structure and development in the language work observed. The HMI study of 1 127 classes from 542 schools in the 7–11 age range (DES, 1978) suggests that more might be done to extend the writing abilities in older and more able pupils, such as in presenting a coherent argument, exploring alternative possibilities, drawing conclusions and making judgements.

The HMI survey of forty-eight 9–13 age range middle schools (DES, 1983) concludes that in general children in this age-range need more opportunities to write for a variety of purposes in a range of styles.

Overall, these and other reports from observational research such as those of the ORACLE studies (Galton *et al.*, 1980) give a broad picture of teaching which is, if anything, over-concerned with basic skills and lacking in a framework which allows for differentiation and development in children's writing.

A framework of writing aims

In my earlier book (Beard, 1984a) I introduced the framework of different writing *aims* drawn from the work of James L. Kinneavy (1971, 1983). Kinneavy's model is based on the so-called communication triangle. Four different aims are identified by locating where the emphasis lies within any act of written communication, on writer, audience, language, or the world to which all can refer.

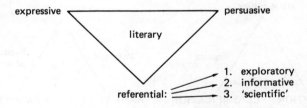

I have provided further details of this model of aims in my book and tried to forge some links between it and the nature of the primary curriculum. In this paper I want to give more attention to another aspect of Kinneavy's work which could be of considerable use in schools in this country, his framework related to *modes* of organisation in writing.

The importance of organisation in writing

We write for different purposes – to convey information, to

make a poem, to persuade others to do things differently. However, in order to fulfil these kinds of aims, we can organise our writing in different ways such as telling a story, describing places, people or things, or evaluating which is the best out of several alternatives. Kinneavy *et al.* (1976) suggest that such modes of organisation represent different 'windows on reality'. They go on to discuss a four-fold model which is close to that used in ancient Greece by Cicero:

> description   – matters of fact
> narrative   – matters of action
> classification – matters of definition
> evaluation   – matters of quality

The distinctive features of each of these modes can be represented diagrammatically:

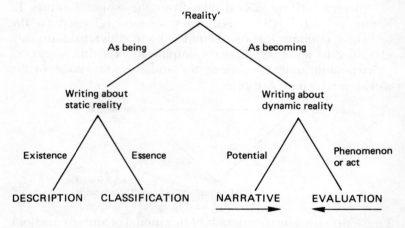

Fundamentally, description and classification are concerned with features of *static* reality, whereas narrative and evaluation are concerned with features of *dynamic* reality. In turn, description focuses on the *existence* of aspects of static reality; classification focuses on the *essence* of these aspects and what distinguishes one from another. Similarly, narrative is centred on *potential* change and the forward-moving release of this potential; evaluation is centred on a *phenomenon or act* in relation to a backward look to what its potential seemed to offer.

Two brief asides need to be made at this point. First,

Kinneavy's framework is a little different from the more common list of the modes of discourse: description, narrative, exposition and argument (see, for example, Britton *et al.*, 1975, pp. 3–5). Kinneavy suggests that argument is better placed in the framework of *aims* (approximating to 'persuasion' therein). He also feels that 'exposition' is too general a term, having several different meanings including all four of the modes set out above.

Second, it is essential to note that the modes are rarely used in isolation, but selectively and eclectically according to the task undertaken and the basic aim for writing. For instance, a typical short story is likely to be dominated by the use of the narrative mode, but is also likely to contain descriptions of settings, classifications of characters and evaluations of themes which run through it.

With these asides in mind, we can now take a closer look at how these modes of organisation can be seen at work in books for children and in children's writing. Before that, though, we need to bear in mind that several recent publications indicate that writing in schools could be made more effective if teachers and children become more aware of the main features of these different modes of writing, especially classification and evaluation.

The HMI survey of primary schools, for example, reports that 'what is written is often descriptive or narrative . . . more children might be expected to develop an argument or to explore an idea when writing than is now the case' (DES, 1978, pp. 111–12). This lack of experience of handling the more 'discursive' modes may account for the findings in the longitudinal research of A. Wilkinson *et al.* (1980). Here it was found that when ten-year-olds were asked to explain things or develop an argument in writing, many of them attempted to apply the narrative mode where it was clearly unsuitable (such as considering whether school attendance should be optional).

Indeed, in a major paper, R. W. Shuy (1981) has argued that out of five language systems relevant to writing (spelling and punctuation; morphology; vocabulary, syntax and written discourse), the latter is likely to be the most important in writing development as children learn to *organise* writing according to circumstances. Certainly the recent paper from HMI is in no doubt about the major factor in children's writing development, that 'they should develop control of written modes appropriate to an increasing range of purposes' (DES, 1984, p. 21). This kind of emphasis on modes can be seen to be especially significant for educators generally in the light of the sudden regeneration of interest and research in the 'second R' (Beard, 1984b). At the recent international writing convention at the University of East Anglia, several eminent speakers seem to struggle to find the most appropriate term of reference for organisation in writing. Many seemed to settle for 'genre'. The latter term is not entirely satisfactory for, according to its Oxford English Dictionary definition, 'genre' is a kind of classification of types of literature (poetry, drama, novel, essay, etc.) rather than of writing in general.

The descriptive mode

As the earlier references to research findings indicate, children are familiar enough with description to be able to adopt it regularly in their writing in the primary school years. Yet we need to think carefully about the distinctive features of the descriptive mode in order to encourage further its use in children's writing.

Written descriptions report on some aspect of the reality of the world as if it were not involved in change and are inevitably selective. The selection and the 'structure of reassembly' in written details will be influenced by different aspects of the communication triangle, the audience of the writer's literal and metaphorical point of view and the context of the writer's aim. We can see these factors at work in the following description of a farm boy from the early part of this century. The unusual use of the present tense here is due to the authors' concern to create maximum verisimilitude.

> Soon, George Woodget comes home. He is twelve but is small for his age. He is wearing a shirt with no collar, a coat several sizes too big with no buttons, and torn, baggy trousers. They are so stiff with meal and mud that they look as if they would stand up on their own. He wears a

shapeless hat with a wide, tattered brim that falls over his eyes. He has no socks, and on his feet are huge boots, caked with mud. It is now twelve o'clock and he has already been working for six hours but as it is Sunday he has finished for the day. He has a job on a dairy farm and cows need milking and feeding every day.

(Speed and Speed, 1980, p. 68)

As well as being supported by several illustrations, this history text is integrated with simulated interviews with the farmer's boy, his father and indeed with many other representative characters from the past. There is particular concern with the audience in this case: the references to the time, the hours already worked and the sardonic comment, 'but as it is Sunday . . .' seems intended to shake a pupil audience into a realisation of working conditions eighty years ago.

The classification mode

Classification involves organising a written text to deal with things as members of groups. This has three distinctive traits – grouping, defining and 'systematising' groups into larger and smaller ones. A central process of this organisation of a static view of reality is deciding on the *range* of definition be it *nominal* (for example, the 'provisional' labels of personality types); *real* (as when we deal with species); or *contextual*, which uses specialised frameworks adopted in subject areas. We can see a specialised framework at work in the following excerpts from an attractive book on volcanoes in Wayland's new 'Planet Earth' series (Carson, 1983). In dealing with 'types of eruptions' the author establishes the basis of his classification:

Despite their differences, eruptions can be divided into several groups which are named after outstanding examples.

Hawaiian eruptions are the quietest of all. Their lava is very runny and the gas can escape easily without explosions . . .

Strombolian eruptions are slightly more violent. They

are named after Stromboli, a tiny volcanic island off Italy which has been erupting frequently for hundreds of years . . .

Whatever the merits of the accuracy and appropriateness of the content of the book, the use of classification mode is made clear by the initial announcement of the range of definition, the use of italics and new paragraphs when dealing with each type, and some very carefully chosen colour photographs.

The narrative mode

In Kinneavy's terms, the narrative mode is essentially concerned with dynamic reality and the movement from potency to actuality. A 'weak' narrative will be little more than a simple chronology. Narrative 'strength', on the other hand, is achieved by exploring the causal links of its components, the complexity of their interaction often building towards some kind of climax and denouement. For example, see these processes at work at the beginning of Florence Parry Heide's (1975) 'The Shrinking of Treehorn':

> Something very strange was happening to Treehorn. The first thing he noticed was that he couldn't reach the shelf in his closet that he had always been able to reach before, the one where he hid his candy bars and bubble gum.
>
> Then he noticed that his clothes were getting too big. 'My trousers are all stretching or something,' said Treehorn to his mother. 'I'm tripping on them all the time.' 'That's too bad, dear,' said his mother, looking into the oven. 'I do hope this cake isn't going to fall,' she said. 'And my sleeves come down way below my hands,' said Treehorn. 'So my shirts must be stretching, too.' 'Think of that,' said Treehorn's mother. 'I just don't know why this cake isn't rising the way it should. Mrs. Abernale's cakes are *always* nice. They *always* rise.' Treehorn started out of the kitchen. He tripped on his trousers, which indeed did seem to be getting longer and longer.
>
> At dinner that night Treehorn's father said, 'Do sit up, Treehorn. I can hardly see your head.' 'I *am* sitting up.'

said Treehorn. 'This is as far up as I come. I think I must be shrinking or something.' 'I'm sorry my cake didn't turn out very well,' said Treehorn's mother.

The evaluative mode

Kinneavy suggests that the evaluation mode is also concerned with 'dynamic' aspects of reality, comparing 'what is or was' with 'what might have been', (what the potential of the phenomena seemed to offer). The major dimensions of an evaluation are likely to include decisions on the 'objects' of the evaluation (actions, artefacts) the 'locus' of the value (be they inherent in the object, part of an agreed 'code' or essentially bound up with someone's attitude); the range of audience; and the method of evaluation (logic, lists, definitions or functions).

In a recent book for primary school children on computers (Litterick and Smithers, 1983), there is a helpful example of evaluative mode in use. To help children begin to think about the implications of new technologies, the authors use, as the 'locus' of the value, two exaggerated stereotypes of the computerised society. 'Computopia' has quickly developing knowledge and skills; a contented workforce working short hours and enjoying a rewarding leisure life; many diseases have been wiped out; crime has been practically wiped out; many sick people are healed – all because of computer systems. 'Computyrannia' on the other hand, has a high number of discontented unemployed people, many of those who do work have dull repetitive jobs, there is escalating social unrest and crime – again all because of the influence of computer systems.

Children reading the book are then encouraged to consider a series of questions as the main 'method' of evaluation, each of which centres on a stem: for example, *Work*: How will we share work with machines and with each other? *Ecology*: How will we use computers to protect and not ruin the world in which we live? Other questions deal with leisure, education and training, privacy, development, and war and peace. The remainder of the book is organised into clearly labelled sections which provide information to help the answering of these questions.

Modes in children's writing

Perhaps the most commonly used mode in children's writing is the narrative. Many children develop a strong narrative sense by a remarkably early age. They seem to internalise very readily a 'story grammar' which may include typical features such as formal beginnings and endings, the use of a central character, events which share the same time and place sequence, the use of the past tense and quotations of speech. Notice how Clare, aged nine, builds these features into here imaginative story:

It began as quite an ordinary day . . .

It began as quite an ordinary day, the sun was shining and the birds were singing. So I decided to go for a walk.

The park was empty so I went to the pond in the middle, then I sat down beside it and looked up at the sky. Then suddenly the pond water started to drain away! 'That's funny' I thought, so I got up and stepped into the empty space and there I saw a tiny little door. I tugged at it and it came open quite easily. Nobody was about so I crawled inside.

When I could stand on my feet again, I had the surprise of my life, it could'nt be true, for there, sitting round a little table were 12 little dwarfs, or elves, or how ever you like to put it.

For a moment I just stood there, with my mouth wide open, speechless. Then I realised what I must look like to them, but they didn't seem to understand my language. They gave me a bowl of . . . well, something like oat-meal. so cautiously I took a spoon-full and it seemed quite nice so I carried on. They seemed quite friendly so I stayed for a while, then one of the dwarfs seemed to want me to go with him. 'Perhaps there'll make me their queen,' I thought. The dwarf led me up some steps and through a door, and to my disappointment I was back where I had started beside the pond. I turned round to thank him but he had disappeared, and the pond was filling up with water.

That night when I lay in bed, I thought 'how strange, just like Alice through the Looking Glass!'

Some commentators have argued that narrative has a unique psychological appeal and therefore should be exploited in educational institutions. Barbara Hardy (1968) reminds us that 'We dream in narrative, day-dream in narrative, remember, anticipate, hope, despair, believe, doubt, plan, revise, criticise, construct, gossip, learn, hate and love by narrative'. The Bullock Report cites the earlier work of F. Whitehead *et al.* (1974) that in the 10–14 age range 'the narrative mode provided for all children by far the strongest motivation towards the reading of books' (Bullock, 1975, p. 129). More recently Barrie Wade (1984) has given an extensive review of how 'story and storying' can be more fully exploited in schools.

The use of the descriptive mode is also well established in schools. It is often interwoven with the use of narrative but can sometimes exist alone, in informative writing and especially in the 'poetic prose' of so-called 'creative writing', as in nine-year-old Martin's piece on 'fog':

Fog

The mystic mist surges round the mystfied trees. The white ghost haunts again among the entangled groves of red yellow brown and green trees. The grass is covered by small strands of cobwebs each blade of grass is joined together by a single silky fringe of cobweb. The visibilty is down to nought and a white ghost reaches up to the sky.

As was suggested earlier, examples of the other kinds of modes, classification and evaluation, do not seem to be so common in schools. Both kinds of writing evolve from where the young writer has to make an *ordered selection* from 'reality', but also a *critical discrimination* between its manifestations. See for example, ten-year-old Paul's use of classification:

Deep water channels are marked by buoys, and the most important buoys are known by a name or a number which will be painted on them. They also mark dangerous sandbanks, wrecks, or other obstructions hidden under the water.

Some buoys are round, some are cone-shaped, and

some are shaped like a can. A can-shaped buoy must be kept to port. A cone-shaped buoy must be kept to starboard, and a globe-shaped buoy may be passed on either side. There is another kind of buoy which is fixed so firmly to the river bed that it is strong enough for a ship to tie up to, instead of dropping her anchor.

Here, Judith, aged twelve, brings off a remarkably mature evaluation of the personality of King John.

King John: Guilty or Innocent?

King John was in my view schizophrenic; he was sharply divided, on one hand he was a good and just king and on the other a powerful tyrant with an insatiable desire for money – and no morals stand between him and it.

A Good King: It must be said King John was at times a brilliant king. In this mood he was quieter than usual, a gentle, scholarly man, a man with a strict sense of write and wrong. He campaigned ceaselessly for peace within his kingdom. Spending most of his time on the move from town to town county to county he founded administrations, settled many disputes, and appointed sheriffs to be responsible for the law. He also made sure his sheriffs weren't above the law . . .

A Cruel Tyrant: The second of Johns personalities was definitely his worse half – a viscous money loving bully – a man who created or perverted the law to his own ends, a ruthless extortionist. There is little doubt that Prince Arthur Richard Ists succesor was killed on John's orders to give him power over the country. He threw many people into jail and indeed tortured them until he extorted sufficient money from him. It was the church's land and money he envied most and he spent a good deal of his time discrediting and stealing from the church.

Summary: I have presented the evidence as I know it. It is however biased as is everything – if not by me by the people who recorded these events centuries ago. John had two different personalities as everyone else does. Much ill was written against him but good also comes through. Is it not possible that he would be remembered with greater affection if he was a warrior like his brother, a man who fought well but neglected his kingdom all through his reign?

Using reading resources in developing children's writing

In what ways can we help strengthen the links between what children read and how they write? Five main principles for practice seem especially important.

1. *Read widely – to the children.* The practice of reading aloud to children is a well-established one in our schools. My guess is, however, that because of the popularity of fiction, much of what is read to children is often in the narrative and descriptive modes, especially in the shape of novels and poetry. The reading of *non-fiction* aloud to children seems far less common and consequently they often do not have the opportunity of experiencing the other modes of classification and evaluation in this way. Thus it seems important not only to continue to read aloud to children of all ages but to do so 'widely', making use of an appropriate range of texts, fiction and non-fiction, and to do so 'purposefully', as the curriculum context suggests it, rather than just for entertainment at the end of the school day.

2. *Alert children to the organisation of texts.* A natural development of reading aloud to children is to encourage them to read for themselves with an alertness to a writer's technique (Bereiter and Scardamalia, 1982, p. 44). Instances of narrative cohesion, the introduction of classification frameworks or effective description can be shared with the class as good examples of the 'how' in writing. K. Perera (1984) provides many examples of the linguistic subtleties involved in the organisation of texts.

3. *Encourage children to 'learn to write by reading'.* Frank Smith (1984) has recently given a new twist to his well known cliché about how children learn to read. Smith argues that in order to become competent writers, children need to read like a writer, in order to learn how to write like a writer. This point of view is

supported by the research of C. Bereiter and M. Scardamalia (1982) whose work with primary school children suggests that in order to fulfil a variety of writing tasks, children need both 'content knowledge' and 'discourse knowledge', that is, how instructions are phrased, arguments developed or stories told. This discourse knowledge includes some under-estimated aspects, for example, the conventional ways to end a piece of writing. Such a perspective suggests two final principles for practice: one connected with the classroom context and the other with the selection of reading resources.

4. *Provide a realistic classroom context.* Insights into discourse knowledge are most likely to come from activities which involve using written language for genuine communicative purposes. In *Children's Writing in the Primary School*, (Beard, 1984a) I have provided nearly fifty examples of children's writing from my own work in primary schools which in most cases reflect authentic involvement of this kind. Even more importantly, I stress the importance of the particular nature of the classroom community which evolves in primary schools. This sense of community can be used in several ways to foster awareness of the modes of writing. Collaborative work, in producing classroom newspapers for example, provide many possibilities for the kinds of drafting, editing and proof-reading which are likely to help children to look more critically at the *organisation* of writing as well as the nuances of vocabulary, spelling and grammar and punctuation. One of the main appeals to children of word-processing facilities is the way in which they *ease* the process of strengthening narrative links, adding details of description, or inserting the topic sentence which clarifies the basis of a classification or evaluation. As I have said elsewhere (Beard, 1984a), on certain occasions the teacher can lead from the front in these sorts of activities, showing the children how he or she would construct a text by writing or typing *in front of the children* and providing the kind of 'process commentary' which is demanded in, for example, the advanced driving test.

5. *Select the right resources for reading.* Running through the whole of this paper is the assumption that the quality of *organisation* in the books which children read can be a major influence in the development of their writing. The obvious implication is that in

assessing the readability of books we need to think far more widely than just in terms of word and sentence length. As C. Harrison (1980) reminds us, aspects of readability within the text can include legibility, illustrations and colour, vocabulary, conceptual difficulty syntax *and* organisation. While we may recognise the more familiar modes of discourse narratives and descriptions, we need also to look at the nature and influence of other modes which occur in subjects across the curriculum. For in selecting books for use in schools, we need to look not only at what these books say, but also how they say it.

References

BEARD, R. (1984a) *Children's Writing in the Primary School* (Sevenoaks: Hodder and Stoughton Educational).

BEARD, R. (1984b) 'The Second R Regenerated?' *The Times Educational Supplement*, 2 November.

BENNETT, N. *et al.* (1984) *The Quality of Pupil Learning Experiences* (London: Lawrence Erlbaum Associates).

BEREITER, C. and SCARDAMALIA, M. (1982) 'From Conversation to Composition: the Role of Instruction in a Developmental Process' in R. Glaser (ed.) *Advances in Instrumental Psychology*, vol. 2 (London: Lawrence Erlbaum Associates).

BRITTON, J. *et al.* (1975) *The Development of Writing Abilities (11–18)* (Basingstoke: Macmillan Education Ltd).

BULLOCK REPORT (1975) *A Language for Life* (London: HMSO).

CARSON, J. (1983) *Volcanoes* (Hove: Wayland Publishers Ltd).

DES (1978) *Primary Education in England* (London: HMSO).

DES (1982) *Education 5 to 9: an illustrative survey of 80 first schools in England* (London: HMSO).

DES (1983) *9–13 Middle Schools: an illustrative survey* (London: HMSO).

DES (1984) *English from 5 to 16* (London: HMSO).

GALTON, M. *et al.* (1980) *Inside the Primary Classroom* (London: Routledge and Kegan Paul Ltd).

HARDY, B. (1968) *The Appropriate Form, an Essay on the Novel* (London: Athlone Press).

HARRISON, C. (1980) *Readability in the Classroom* (Cambridge University Press).

HEIDE, F. P. (1975) *The Shrinking of Treehorn* (Harmondsworth: Penguin (Puffin) Books).

KINNEAVY, J. L. (1971) *A Theory of Discourse* (Englewood Cliffs, New Jersey: Prentice-Hall).

KINNEAVY, J. L. (1983) 'A pluralistic synthesis of four contemporary models for teaching composition' in A. Freedman *et al.* (eds) *Learning to Write: First Language/Second Language* (London: Longman).

KINNEAVY, J. L. *et al.* (1976) *Writing: Basic Modes of Organisation* (Dubuque, Iowa: Kendall Hunt Publishing Co.).

LITTERICK, I. and SMITHERS, C. (1983) *Computers and You* (Hove: Wayland Publishers Ltd).

PERERA, K. (1984) *Children's Writing and Reading* (Oxford: Basil Blackwell).

SHUY, R. W. (1981) 'Towards a Developmental Theory of Writing' in C. H. Frederiksen and J. F. Dominic (eds) *Writing: The Nature, Development and Teaching of Written Communication*, vol. 2 (Hillsdale, New Jersey: Lawrence Erlbaum Associates).

SMITH, F. (1984) *Reading Like a Writer* (Centre for the Teaching of Reading, University of Reading).

SPEED, P. and M., (1980) *The Modern Age* (Oxford Junior History 5) (Oxford University Press by arrangement with the BBC).

WADE, B. (1984) *Story at Home and School*, Educational Review Occasional Publications no. 10 (University of Birmingham).

WILKINSON, A. *et al.* (1980) *Assessing Language Development* (Oxford University Press).

WHITEHEAD, F. *et al.* (1974) *Children's Reading Interests*, Schools Council Working Paper no. 52 (Evans/Methuen Educational).

Chapter 15

The Expression of Feeling in Stories Written by Children

Helen Cowie

Investigations into children's narrative writing vary enormously in their emphasis. Some consider aspects of writing process, writer–audience relationship, or the context within which good writing takes place; others analyse the end-product in terms of structure, qualities of the characters in a story or the degree of social sensitivity expressed by the young writer. Is it possible to integrate insights about writing process with the evaluation of the end-product? In this paper I argue that it is. I also argue that the teacher is in a unique position to understand the many factors which contribute to a child's story.

Writing: process or product?

The variety of new books and articles on the subject of children's writing indicates a burgeoning of recent research into the development of writing abilities. However, for the teacher who is interested in applying these findings to the classroom there are problems. First, there is still no general theory of writing development, and controversies over what is good writing and how best it may be facilitated, still abound. Secondly, although the range of disciplines from which studies of writing are drawn – English, Education, Psychology, Linguistics – has resulted in some cross-fertilisation of ideas, there are still many barriers and misunderstandings.

Let's look first at some studies which focus on the writing process, the writer/audience relationship and the particular context which a writer needs if fluency is to be achieved and meaning expressed. Themes include the complex relationship between writer, audience and writing environment; the shift from egocentrism to audience awareness; and the encouragement of child control of the writing process. D. H. Graves (1983) for example, suggests that children readily draft, revise and edit their own writing when they are working in the context of a writing community in which trust, sharing of ideas and 'conferencing' with fellow-writers are an integral part of the writing process, and the authentic expression of the individual's 'voice'.

Although this type of research uses small numbers of subjects and is limited in the extent to which broad generalisations can be drawn from it, it does provide a useful perspective on children's development as writers. The findings are rich in observations, pupil-teacher dialogues and ongoing thoughts of children as they write or plan. These studies tend to take place in naturalistic settings and are often carried out by researchers who are experienced as teachers of writing themselves. One of the most influential researchers in this category has been J. N. Britton whose developmental model differentiates 'transactional' and 'poetic' writing modes each with a common origin in the 'expressive' mode. His ideas have had enormous influence on educational practice in this country and he has encouraged teachers to make a shift from the transactional type of writing so predominant in the secondary school curriculum (Britton *et al.*, 1975; Bullock Report, 1975) to the personal, poetic type of writing which, he claims, fosters personal growth and sensitivity to others, and also helps writers understand experiences more fully.

However, criticisms have been made of Britton's model (Griffiths and Wells, 1983; Wilkinson, Barnsley, Hanna and Swan, 1980) and it is likely that his two-fold distinction between the transactional and the poetic may be an over-simplification.

M. Griffiths and G. Wells (1983), for example, studying adult writing, note a great variability in their subjects' use of informal, expressive writing as an aid to thinking for both transactional and poetic purposes, and they question whether Britton's two categories are mutually exclusive. Clearly more rigorous testing of these ideas needs to be carried out.

Even more than Britton, Graves (1983) relies heavily on

case-study material, despite the fairly large number of children in his sample. By the nature of his approach, which is deliberately planned not to interfere with normal classroom activities or with the writing development of individual children, Graves' data cannot be subjected to rigorous analysis; it is difficult to compare one child with another. His assertions about the value of giving the *child* control of the writing process, for example, are supported by observations of individual children as they write, and by the richness of his own experience as teacher.

Many teachers respond with enthusiasm to Graves' ideas, but some remain cautious in accepting such statements in the absence of systematic evidence. Do we really know that by expressing themselves through personal and poetic-writing modes, children come to understand themselves and others more fully? If this does occur, does the writing achieve it or is it part of a developmental process which is happening anyway? How effective is the 'conference' compared to more traditional methods? What precisely is 'voice'?

Perhaps we need to complement intensive observations of individual children as they write with analyses of the writing which they produce. The most common design for research of this type has involved giving children of different ages the same writing task and then comparing the results. This can be done by analysing *structural* properties of narratives (Kroll and Anson, 1984; Stein and Goldman, 1981). B. Kroll and C. Anson, using the story grammar method of analysis, argue that structural complexity tends to be related to the complexity of the goals, motivations and responses of the characters in a narrative:

> The deeper these qualities of characterisation become, the greater is the need to structure the story in a complex way.
>
> (p. 169)

The ability to structure a story has also been shown to be something which improves with age (Cowie, 1985).

Alternatively, by focusing directly on *emotional* expression in the writing of seven-, ten- and thirteen-year-old children, A. Wilkinson and his colleagues on the Crediton Project (Wilkinson, *et al.*, 1980) find an age-related trend in the ability of children to express feeling (or 'affect', as they call it) in the characters of their narratives. The authors argue that their study, closely based on Piaget's stages of development, demonstrates decentering of self, and a growing awareness of other people (including the reader of the story). They note the great difference between *speech* with its gestures, inflections, intonation and face-to-face interaction, and *writing*, where children have to rely on stylistic devices to convey feeling.

However, A. Wilkinson and his colleagues fail to acknowledge the effect of context on the child's ability to decentre (Borke, 1971; Donaldson, 1978; Hughes and Donaldson, 1983). Nor do they refer to the influence of role-taking activities such as fantasy play, drama and story-telling on the growing capacity of young children to take on the perspective of other people and empathise with their feelings (Scarlett and Wolf, 1979; Galda, 1984). These abilities have been shown by many researchers to develop throughout the pre-school and infant school years.

Is integration possible?

Most of us would agree that the end product is only part of a process in which young writers try to make links between experiences, real or imagined, rich in excitement and emotion, on the one hand and external communicative language on the other. In Britton's words, the child seems to be 'structuring the web of meaning' rather than simply searching for words which reflect an event.

But how do we evaluate what is happening? Can we integrate the insights which studies of writing process have given us with the more objective data of product-oriented research? I believe that we can, and I believe that the teacher is in a unique position to understand the intentions of the child and the context within which a particular piece of writing is produced. I discuss this more fully in my book (Cowie, 1984).

The role of the conference

Graves argues that the young child, like the accomplished

author, can learn to view a piece as a draft which can be worked on and improved. The key to this is 'ownership'; children can develop control over their own writing processes, provided that the voice which is being expressed is authentic and the audience unthreatening. From this it follows that, where possible, children should be encouraged to write about topics of interest to *them*, not topics imposed by the teacher.

The concept of the conference which grew out of Graves' New Hampshire Study, refers to the short interview between teacher and children where sensitive, concerned questions are asked and where the young writers are enabled to express more effectively the meanings which they intend to convey. The important thing about the conference is that the teacher follows the child. As a result of his observations of many conferences, Graves (1983, pp. 227–8) recommends the teacher to:

> ask questions they think the child can answer, help the child to focus; and give the child space and time to find his or her own voice.

The method, it seems to me, owes much to the client-centred techniques of therapists like Carl Rogers. Here is an example of a conference (Graves, 1983, pp. 100–1):

Conference One

Ms Jacobs: How is the writing going, Rodney?

Rodney: OK.

Ms Jacobs: Tell me what your piece is about. (The teacher deliberately lets Rodney keep his paper and chat about it.)

Rodney: Well, it's about my dog, Nicky. He's pretty loud.

Ms Jacobs: So he makes a lot of noise and bothers you?

Rodney: Yeah, he barks like crazy. Sometimes it bothers me but the bad part is the neighbors don't like it.

Ms Jacobs: The neighbors are upset?

Rodney: They've called the police a couple of times. But the dog can't help it. He was beaten when he was little. That's before we got him. We don't beat him. But that's why he barks so much.

> Ms Jacobs: Sort of makes you wonder what will happen next. What can you do?
> Rodney: Well, you can't beat him some more. We could put a muzzle on but that's cruel.
> Ms Jacobs: And you've been writing about all this?
> Rodney: Most of it.
> Ms Jacobs: Is there anything you need help with?
> Rodney: I think I'm okay.
> Ms Jacobs: (Final receiving goes here.)

Four further examples illustrate how conferences can help the child reveal feelings which are not always apparent in the writing (Cowie, 1985).

The feelings which underlie children's writing

Take nine-year-old Owen's piece about war in space:

SPACE WAR

I'm in a ray machine
Being attacket
Lazer's out of order
I'm loosing power
Engines on full blast
Speeding froo space
Glowing red hot
I land on space station S7, 1
We send out troupes of armed shuttles
The enemy is driven away
I go to the food despenser and get some fish and chips

A short conference reveals that Owen is not happy about this piece, especially the hurried ending. From being a highly imaginative writer, he has quite suddenly become uninspired; the ideas won't come any more. 'I recently stopped writing. I don't like writing any more. Mostly I just think.' Not long ago his baby brother was born and he is feeling left out at home. Perhaps he will want to write about those thoughts, perhaps not, but he knows that his teacher understands something of what he is going through at the moment. In context, the piece takes on new meaning.

Claire, also aged nine, writes about the day a baby sparrow finds his mother dead. The sparrow shows no emotional reaction to the event:

FLIGHT

A baby sparrow waiting for his lunch, finds his mother dead on the grass he flaps his wings and for the first he rises out of the nest and flies away over the hills then he stops for a rest on top of a tree he spots a lonely nest and settles down for the night.

On Wilkinson's scale, she would make a low score for the expression of affect. However, the conference shows that Claire is really exploring her own feelings about solitude, free from pressures of family life. She *can* enter into the baby sparrow's experience and take his perspective on the world; she can contrast the calm of the sparrow's flight with the bustle of everyday life. She says:

> I like this piece because I like thinking about the sky and the lovely sky and the colours of the sky, and it's a nice view from up where you are to where they are on the ground. I like thinking about the clouds and if *I* was floating in the air – quiet, lonely. You have to stay in the air all the time and couldn't go down to where all the things were going on. It's quiet on your own – no one to bother you, like brothers and sisters.

Sometimes children will use a story to experiment with responses to a situation and see the outcome. This is a safe way of acting out emotion. Here eleven-year-old Peter describes some of the anger he felt when he was given the wrong change in a newsagent's shop:

AN ANGRY MORNING

One day I went to a shop to buy a comic which cost nine pence. When I gave the money to the lady at the counter she gave me one pence change but I had given her fifty pence. The lady at the counter thought that I had given her ten pence but when I explained to her that I had given her fifty pence she didn't give my proper change. My head nearly blew off in anger so to get my own back I pushed over a stand with crisps in which made me much better.

The conference shows how he has fantasised about showing the anger which he did not dare express at the time. 'I did the 50p bit but I didn't push over the crisps. I went to the shop once and somebody tripped and pushed them over so I thought I'd put that in.' He is not really happy with the piece: 'It's just a description saying what happened', but still expresses anger by going red and tensing his hands as he remembers the incident. The piece has not done full justice to the emotions which he felt but talking about it may help him next time when he tries to recapture a painful experience.

Andrew, aged eleven, has had trouble in writing his piece about being afraid in the dark:

FRIGHTENED
When I am frightened its because when I come at of the loo I tern the light off. Then I get a funy fierling that there is a man at the window. My hart was frobing I felt like a Steem train gon cold.

However, the conference shows how much emotion has in fact been involved in this writing:

I still do feel like that but it's going away a bit. I *am* scared of the dark but I don't admit it. My Mum and Dad say 'You big baby!' when it's thundery and I go downstairs, but I don't admit it now. I *look* brave but I'm not feeling brave, just scared.

He adds:

Writing it brought all the frightening things back to me and I feel cold and frightened again.

From the piece alone it would be hard to guess how much the child was feeling. The conference offers the teacher one way of sharing Andrew's experience and perhaps enabling him to come to terms with his fear.

Conclusion

Objective studies of the content of children's stories indicate a directly age-related sequence of development from literal, unemotional writing (in infants and first year juniors) to writing which shows insight, empathy and an awareness of emotions in self and others. However, conversations with young writers reveal a different pattern. The written words of younger children have often, it is true, failed to capture the wealth of emotions which underlie them, but conferences seem to show that all children use some of their narrative at least as one means of increasing their understanding of social and emotional issues in their own lives.

To read the stories without talking to the authors often means missing some important intention or emotion on the part of the child. The receptivity of the reader seems to me to be a crucial element in the process of writing; this is the area where response to the story and knowledge of the child interact with the actual content of the narrative. And it is this interaction between child and teacher which so strongly influences the direction which the child's narrative competence will take.

Suggested discussion issues

Here is a short list of suggested discussion issues which could be raised during individual conference sessions. I would like to thank Mrs Lynn Griffiths for allowing me to reproduce these discussion points which she has been using in conferences with her class.

How are things going this morning?
What is the main thing you're trying to say?
Who is the most important person in your story?
Could you describe him/her a bit more?
Which do you think is the most important part of your story?
Read to me the part you're pleased with.
Read to me your favourite piece in your story
Tell me what you really like about that bit.
Read to me any bits that you feel unhappy about.
Is there anything that doesn't seem to fit into the rest of your story?
Are there any pieces you could describe more? I can't quite picture it.

Is there any other way you could order the things that happen?
Is what you're telling me important to you?
Where did you get your main idea from?
What is important to you in your story?
Can you tell me what is going to happen next?

References

BORKE, H. (1971) 'Interpersonal perception of young children: egocentrism or empathy?' *Developmental Psychology*, no. 5, pp. 263–9.

BRITTON, J. N. BURGESS, T., MARTIN. N., McLEOD, A. and ROSEN, H. (1975) *The Development of Writing Abilities 11–18* (London: Macmillan).

BULLOCK REPORT (1975) *A Language for Life* (London: HMSO).

COWIE, H. (ed.) (1984) *The Development of Children's Imaginative Writing* (London: Croom Helm).

COWIE, H. (1985) *An Approach to the Evaluation of Children's Narrative Writing* (Unpublished PhD thesis, University of London Institute of Education).

DONALDSON, M. (1978) *Children's Minds* (London: Fontana).

GALDA, L. (1984) 'Narrative competence: play, story-telling and story-comprehension', in A. Pellegrini and T. Yawkey (eds) *The Development of Oral and Written Language in Social Contexts* (Norwood, New Jersey: Ablex).

GRAVES, D. H. (1983) *Writing: Teachers and Children at Work* (Exeter, New Hampshire: Heinemann).

GRIFFITHS, M. and WELLS, G. (1983) 'Who writes what and why', in B. Kroll and G. Wells (eds) *Explorations in the Development of Writing* (Chichester: John Wiley).

HUGHES, M. and DONALDSON, M. (1983) 'The use of hiding games for studying co-ordination of viewpoints', in M. Donaldson, R. Grieve and B. Pratt (eds) *Early Childhood Development and Education* (Oxford: Basil Blackwell).

KROLL, B. and ANSON, C. (1983) 'Analysing structure in children's fictional narratives', in H. Cowie (ed.) *The Development of Children's Imaginative Writing*.

SCARLETT, G. and WOLF, D. (1979) 'When it's only make believe: the construction of a boundary between fantasy and reality in story-telling', in H. Gardner and E. Winner (eds) *Fact Fiction and Fantasy in Childhood* (San Francisco: Jossey Bass).

STEIN, N. and GOLDMAN, S. R. (1981) 'Children's knowledge about social situations', in S. R. Asher and J. M. Gottman (eds) *The Development of Children's Friendships* (Cambridge University Press).

WILKINSON, A., BARNSLEY, G., HANNA, P. and SWANN, M. (1980) *Assessing Language Development* (Oxford University Press).

Chapter 16

Establishing Cohesion in Children's Writing: The Advantages of Multi-media Instruction Packages

L. John Chapman and Jonathan Anderson

In essence it is proposed that teachers should adopt an approach that envisages reading and writing as complementary activities so that one language facet is not divided from another but rather their reciprocity should be emphasised. Next it is suggested that this fundamental teaching procedure is supported by a multi-media resource, not only of the book but of the cassette player and microcomputer whose dynamic and storage qualities can be exploited to the full by teachers. Experience at the Open University shows that such multi-media approaches need to be planned so that the various constituents are not thought of as isolated elements but integrated into a package to support teaching. To achieve the advantages that such packages offer, it is important that the strengths of each element should be exploited so as to make their qualities count. The elements are:

- *the theoretical advances of cohesion and register*
- *the dynamism of the microcomputer and its storage capacity*
- *the cassette for register listening activities*
- *the children's own writing output*
- *the children's reading of both fiction and factual materials*

Many proposals for the improvement of the teaching of reading and writing have been made down the years and readers will be forgiven if they think that this is just one more. However, we believe that the one we propose here has distinct theoretical and practical advantages over any other.

In the first place, the proposal is grounded on theoretical concepts that are applicable across the age ranges that are met with during the years of compulsory schooling. This is new, for as far as we are aware the linguistic concepts of cohesion and register that allow uniformity of application have not been proposed in this form in educational settings before. This is not surprising as they have only recently been propounded in a form that teachers can implement (Halliday and Hasan, 1976 and 1980; Halliday, 1985; Chapman, 1983). The advantage of having basic concepts that can unify the teaching of both primary and secondary schools is exciting for it could lead to that continuity of teaching, the lack of which is one of today's most pressing problems.

The transition between primary and secondary schools, for example, has been found to be crucial for literacy development. This was made clear by the research of E. A. Lunzer and K. Gardner (1979) who identified the problem. Now the longitudinal research at The Open University has provided further conformation of their findings and the extent of its seriousness. These research findings show that the lack of progress in reading of average and below-average students' attainment during the first year at secondary school as shown by Lunzer and Gardner (1979) rarely improves throughout secondary education. To remedy such a situation, therefore, will require the co-operation and understanding of both primary and secondary teachers. A great deal of rethinking is needed of the kind suggested in this paper.

The task, then, is very great and the changes involved would seem daunting if it were not for the new tools produced by modern technology which can be pressed into service. In particular, the rapid advance of microcomputer technology as indicated in Chapman (1985) has considerable potential which is, as yet, unrealised. In this paper we intend to illustrate how the combination of new theoretical advances in linguistics integrated with the new technologies can give a considerable assistance to the busy teacher. But first some evidence from writing research which supports the importance of the concepts of cohesion.

Research into writing and cohesion

This aspect of cohesion research has not received much attention in this country and apart from a few studies like that of P. Rutter and B. Raban (1982), for example, little has been done. This is not to say that there is no interest in writing in this country, but rather that certain lines of research have not been taken up. And yet, if we adopt a model of reading and writing that envisages them as both sides of the same coin, a teaching position developed later in this paper, then the place of cohesion in the reading process might be informed by research into writing.

Research has been done, however, in the USA, where a number of studies have been carried out into the relationship between three factors: writing quality, cohesion and coherence. The definition of writing quality that is often used in this research can be traced back to the Scottish philosopher Alexander Bain, who in 1866 categorised prose discourse into four modes: description, narration, exposition and persuasion. He stipulated that writing quality consisted of unity, emphasis and coherence. The term coherence, however, is ill-defined, making the distinction between it and cohesion problematic. Coherence has been used as a general term and in some cases almost equivalent to cohesion. There is still a great deal to be done in research to delineate these variables, not the least of the task being to interpret one 'authority' to another. For example, S. P. Witte and L. Faigley (1981) state that Halliday and Hasan do not take real-world settings into consideration. On the contrary they do – Halliday has often stressed the point that meaning is dependent on its situation of context. Halliday has recently put the relationship between cohesion and coherence thus:

> For a text to be coherent, it must be cohesive; but it must be more besides. It must display the resources of cohesion in ways that are motivated by the register of which it is an instance; it must be semantically appropriate with lexico-grammatical realizations to match (i.e. it must make sense); and it must have structure.
>
> (Halliday, 1985)

None the less Witte and Faigley state their position positively:

> Clearly, cohesion analyses measure more sophisticated aspects of language development than do error analyses or syntactic analyses. Cohesion analyses also give us some concrete ways of addressing some of the differences which heretofore could not be explained either to ourselves or to our students in any but the most abstract ways.
>
> (Witte and Faigley, 1981)

This line of research was followed up by G. A. McCulley (1983), who examined the validity of these three factors in writing. In technical terms he sought evidence as to the construct validity of coherence with writing quality and as to the concurrent validity of cohesion in the persuasive mode of discourse. He worked with a sample of 493 papers from the 2 784 persuasive papers written by seventeen-year-olds during 1978–79 national writing assessment by the National

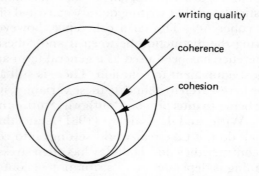

SOURCE: McCulley, 1983.
Coherence explains 41% of the variance in writing quality scores when manuscript length is held constant.
Cohesion explains 53% of the variance in coherence scores when manuscript length is held constant.

FIGURE 16.1   *The relationships among writing quality, coherence, and cohesion based on the findings of McCulley study*

Assessment of Educational Progress (NAEP). McCulley reports that:

> Within the context of the writing assessed in this study (17-year-olds writing persuasively to an authoritative audience), the evidence suggests that coherence, but not textual cohesion is a valid construct of judged writing quality; although the evidence is not as strong as when manuscript length is held constant.

However, as to the position of cohesion as a sub-element within coherence McCulley points out that his evidence on this is inconclusive when manuscript length is held constant. He found that 'textual cohesion might be a far more important attribute of coherence than it is presently considered'. The findings are represented graphically in Figure 16.1.

There is still a great deal to be done in research to clarify these factors, as indicated earlier, but what evidence there is would support that attention to cohesion in children's writing would pay pedagogic dividends.

Teaching the new concepts

In a paper presented to the 20th UKRA Conference held at Worcester, Chapman (1984) presented a four-pronged teaching strategy to improve the teaching of reading and writing. The strategy, which applies to all age-ranges, consists of:

1. Teach reading and writing together.
2. Teach for prediction in reading and writing.
3. Be at least one step ahead.
4. Teach texture, that is,
    (a) Teach for internal text unity (Cohesion)
    (b) Teach for the appropriacy of the text with its situation. (Register).

In the first of these, teaching reading and writing together, Chapman intended to convey a new dimension for the teaching of writing or text construction. It was hoped that the relationship between reading and writing would be explored to the full by children from the start. That is, children should be treated as authors constructing meaningful and important messages that they wish to convey to others who are not present at the time. This is an important perspective to adopt from the beginning for the requirement to write was born of the need to extend communication beyond the here and now. There are, of course, other motivational factors like relevancy and personal satisfaction, but the nature of the process that the children are engaged in needs continual emphasis and explication.

The second prong is concerned with prediction. It has been said that for us to understand each other when we are talking requires the ability to predict what the other is about to say. In the same way, to understand what we are reading involves predicting what the author is about to say. This is a large part of fluency. Activities that encourage prediction therefore, are welcomed and again, should be taught from the beginning. In writing, this principle holds, for writers are predicting what they are going to write as they are writing.

The third strategy is that the teacher needs to be one step ahead of the children's present stage of development. This is desirable from many points of view but in particular there is every chance that if reading has had the attention it deserves it will be leading, or appear to be ahead of, the writing process.

The fourth part of the strategy is to teach texture. This is the new component and at first, because of its novelty, probably the most difficult. Texture, according to M. A. K. Halliday and R. Hasan (1976, 1980; and Halliday, 1985) consists of two major concepts: cohesion and register. The former is concerned with the internal unity of the text and is realised by the cohesive tie system and the latter is concerned with the unity of the text with its situation of context. Register has three dimensions: the Field of Discourse (what the text is about), its Tenor (that is, its appropriacy to the Field in question), and its Mode or channel of communication – for example, whether the text is spoken or written. These constituents of register were discussed briefly in Chapman (1984) and are explained more fully in Chapman and Louw (1986).

These briefly are the new concepts that inform the four-pronged teaching strategy; what follows is an outline of how teachers might approach using the strategy using a combination of media. We examine first the possibilities of using the microcomputer in achieving some of the teaching aims that would be involved in such a programme.

The microcomputer as a tool for writing

When the microcomputer was first introduced into schools there was little software available for teachers to use. After a while a variety of provisions, including some commercially produced, became available and J. Anderson (1984) was able to detect three different kinds of usage. One of these envisaged the creative integration of the microcomputer into the activities provided for children's literacy development. An example of how this might be done has been given by Chapman (1985). In this illustration the microcomputer was used to demonstrate the way in which an author uses cohesive chains to keep track of people and things. This capability is unique, for in no other way can we mirror the dynamic quality of the reading process. And here we come to a major point for this approach. The children are able to work on simple texts provided on the screen and then can be encouraged to look at their own work to check whether they have made their writing hang together. It is then only a small step to begin composing on the microcomputer starting with programs that emulate, for example, the Breakthrough method of beginning writing (Weston, 1984) on the screen. The advantage of this facility is most impressive, as both teacher and child can increment the word banks that are built up when working with this program. Furthermore, by developing the program, it is possible to move quickly from the sentence to text. This is most desirable, as we rarely communicate in single sentences. Indeed, when children are asked for their 'news' they are more likely to give a piece of text rather than a sentence. On the screen they can make meaning using text and they will need to draw on the cohesive elements to do it. The teacher, seeing this progress, will be ready to update the word banks by including some of the cohesive factors appropriate to the child's needs. As the work proceeds through the school, children will move into word-processing which will prepare them for future work in school and on into adult life.

Further work on the computer is envisaged in other areas, for example the prediction strategy noted above. A recent program written by Anderson (1981) provides a further very useful facility which among other things can help teachers achieve this. This program, GAPMAKER . . . GAPTAKER, is a very powerful authoring system which allows teachers to create a whole variety of reading and language activities from stories entered into the computer. They can have separate disks for different topics or for different groups of children or for individual children. The program is very versatile, allowing the teacher to create gaps in the text.

The disk already holds a number of stories but teachers have the option of entering their own stories or, just as importantly, letting children write and then enter their own. These stories, teacher- or child-originated, can now become the texts used for gap-making. A further important point to be made here is that children need to become attuned to differences in register quite early, as they begin to appreciate the purposes of writing. This is important, not only in its own right but because there are variations in cohesive patterns according to both style and register (Gutwinski, 1976; Binkley, 1983). Writing on the computer adds a motivating force as children can produce a finished document that can be sent to people in various walks of life. In doing this they become accustomed to the variations in language required to pass meaningful messages. It is also possible to exploit the use of cassettes containing recordings of different kinds of tests which can be heard by the children individually or in groups. In this way they can become attuned to register variation at an early age, and there is considerable potential here for reading and writing in different registers to develop across the primary school age-range thus avoiding the register shock that presently occurs in the secondary school.

References

ANDERSON, J. (1981) *Gapmaker . . . Gaptaker* (computer program). Available from Flinders University, South Australia.

ANDERSON, J. (1984) 'The Computer as tutor, tutee, tool in reading and language', Reading No. 18, pp. 67–78.

BINKLEY, M. R. (1983) 'A Descriptive and Comparative Study of Cohesive Structure in Text Materials from Differing Academic Disciplines' (Unpublished PhD dissertation, Graduate School of Education, The George Washington University).

CHAPMAN, L. J. (1983) *Reading Development and Cohesion* (London: Heinemann Educational).

CHAPMAN, L. J. (1984) 'Nurturing every child's literacy development: a four-pronged teaching strategy', in D. Dennis (ed.) *Reading and Meeting Children's Special Needs* (London: Heinemann Educational).

CHAPMAN, L. J. (1985) 'Cohesion and the Micro', in J. Ewing (ed.) *Reading and the New Technologies* (London: Heinemann Educational).

CHAPMAN, L. J. and LOUW, W. (1986) 'Register Development and Secondary School Texts', in B. Gillham (ed.), *The Language of School Subjects* (London: Heinemann Educational).

GUTWINSKI, W. (1976) *Cohesion in Literary Texts* (The Hague: Mouton).

HALLIDAY, M. A. K. and HASAN, R. (1976) *Cohesion in English* (London: Longman).

HALLIDAY, M. A. K. and HASAN, R. (1980) *Text and Contexts: Language in a social semiotic perspective* (Sophia Linguistics VI) (Tokyo: Graduate School of Language and Linguistics, Sophia University).

HALLIDAY, M. A. K. (1985) *An Introduction to Functional Grammar* (London: Edward Arnold).

LUNZER, E. A. and GARDNER, K. (1979) *The Effective Use of Reading* (London: Heinemann Educational).

McCULLEY, G. A. (1983) *Writing quality, coherence and cohesion*, D. of Ed. dissertation, Utah State University (Utah: U.S.A.).

RUTTER, P. and RABAN, B. (1982) 'The development of cohesion in children's writing: a preliminary investigation', *First Language*, 3, pp. 63–75.

WESTON, B. (1984) 'Write to Read' (Unpublished M.Ed. Dissertation, Middlesex Polytechnic, London).

WITTE, S. P. and FAIGLEY, L. (1981) 'Coherence, cohesion and writing quality', *College Composition and Communication*, no. 32, pp. 189–204.

Chapter 17

The Computer as a Resource for Teaching Reading: Now and Tomorrow

Joan Feeley

The purpose of this paper is to describe how the microcomputer can be used as a tool and tutor in the teaching or reading. Word processing for reading and writing, utility program for creating materials, readability programs, and filing/database systems are some of the presently available, worthwhile, tool applications that are discussed. Uses of the computer as a tutor for developing reading strategies are also examined. Innovative software programs for these tutor applications, many still in developmental stages, are described as promising resources for the future.

Over the past few years, reading teachers in American schools have been cautious in approaching the microcomputer as a resource for the teaching of reading. Perhaps this is because computers emerged from the field of mathematics with its stress on teach, practice, and test to mastery. In fact, this same model was applied to early software developed for reading and language arts. Since the model works best for providing drill and practice on discrete skills, a plethora of programs was developed to provide exercises at the letter, word and sentence level. D. P. Reinking (1984) found that 70 per cent of the reading/language arts programs in the Microsift database dealt with single letter/single word skills; of 105 programs only seven offered whole text. A. Rubin and B. Bruce (1984) found that only 21 of 317 packages they reviewed required students to read whole text. Hence, the computer was dubbed 'the electronic workbook' by many teachers concerned with reading/language teaching and found more favour in remedial labs or reading centres than in developmental classrooms.

However, the situation seems to be changing. Carl B. Smith (1985) reports that, in percentage use of computers in elementary schools, reading now holds the number two position (49 per cent) below arithmetic (74 per cent). The patterns of use that he notes seem to reflect the current state of the art in software production; 68 per cent of elementary school use is for drill and practice. The computer can serve teachers of reading as more than merely an innovative practice medium. This paper would like to explore some ways the computer may be used as tool and as tutor, in both developmental and remedial settings, both now and in the immediate future.

The computer as a tool

Besides helping teachers to do a myriad of mundane record-keeping tasks and everyday lesson preparation, the computer can serve as a valuable classroom tool in the teaching of reading and writing. Word processing, utility packages that can help teachers tailor their own computer-assisted lessons, readability programs and filing systems are all tool applications available to teachers now. Once learned, they can make the teachers' job of teaching and the student's job of learning easier and more interesting.

Word processing

Word processing (WP) is the general term for software packages that permit the writing, editing, storing and printing of text. It is made to order for teachers who use the Language Experience Approach (LEA) with beginning readers at any level. To use LEA, the teacher draws on a student's experiences to elicit language which is then written down to be read back by the student. The content is then assured to be within the reader's schemata. The teacher writes the text on charts, on the blackboard, or on paper and uses it to teach concepts about reading (letters, words, sentences, directionality, and so forth). Students usually read the stories with the teacher and often take home copies to practice reading by themselves. WP is a perfect vehicle for this approach. As students generate language about their experiences, the teacher can type it straight into the computer. The text can be read back immediately from the screen, stored on disk, and printed out for the student to take away; the teacher can call up the story to work on during later sessions.

To illustrate, I would like to share with you how we used this approach with a remedial reader in our college reading centre. Bill, a second grader, dictated a story about causing a fire in a neighbour's leaf-filled backyard on a warm, autumn day as he was on his way home from school. Knowing that playing with matches was forbidden, he tried to share the guilt with a friend named Jack, saying that they had both started the fire and that it had spread quickly through the crisp, dry leaves; apparently, it turned out to be much bigger than they had anticipated. Fortunately, the neighbour arrived home from work in the nick of time and doused the flames with the garden hose. To teach the boys a lesson, the neighbour gave them a long lecture on the hazards of starting a fire and made them sign pledges saying that they would never do anything like this again.

When Bill returned the next week, it was easy to retrieve his story which had been stored on disk. He had forgotten to bring his copy, but he did bring a paper on which he had pencilled the neighbour's name, telling us that his mother had said we had misspelled it. This was easy to change with the find/change option on our WP program.

Bill had been having trouble with the sight words *were* and *where*, so we decided to work on them in context. Only *were* came up highlighted when we searched the text. He read the word alone and in the sentences with no difficulty. Next he told us that he had actually started the fire himself with Jack standing by reluctantly. As we set about to find *we* to change it to *I*, a syntax problem arose: we had to change the verbs and objective pronouns to make the text sound right and to make sense.

Finally, Bill decided that he would rather begin his story with the last paragraph to make it more exciting. This was easy to do with WP. When we printed out the story the second time, it had all the changes we had made and looked perfect. The dynamic capabilities of WP enabled us to manipulate the text in front of the learner while teaching him a good deal about the writing/reading processes.

Recently I had a five-year-old guest at my home for a few days, giving me a first-hand opportunity to write and read with a beginner at my home computer. Fascinated with WP, Matt continually exhorted me to 'let him type'. One evening, as we returned home from a park concert, we saw the Goodyear Blimp, an advertising dirigible, hovering over our house. With its multicoloured lights flashing designs and messages, it looked like something from outer space to Matt. In his own imaginative mind it was a spaceship, and he could hardly wait to get inside to record this wondrous event. Despite the hour, he pleaded to work at the computer.

First, he planned his composition by telling me just what he wanted to say. Next he typed the words as I spelled for him. He wrote:

> Aunt Joan, Uncle Robbie, Aunt Mary, and Matthew saw a spaceship in the sky on the night of July 3, 1985. It said, 'Welcome to River Edge, Matthew'.

As soon as it was printed out, he added his drawing of a brightly coloured spaceship, with tail rockets streaming, as if thrusting the ship heavenward. The story was continued the next day, with the ship returning to pick up an earthly passenger named Matthew, of course. By the time he returned home, he had three instalments to read to his younger sisters!

So you see, children, too, quickly learn to use this new writing tool. Although accounts of five- and six-year-olds using WP in school have appeared in the literature (Phenix and Hannan, 1984), I have observed mainly older students (nine years to adult) writing at computer terminals. The concept of WP fits very well in classrooms in which writing as a process (Graves, 1983; Calkins, 1983) is practised. According to the process approach, writers take a text through many stages: drafting, revising, editing and finally publishing a perfect copy to be read by others. Teachers at all levels who encourage a process approach are quick to see the advantages of access to WP. Usually, the early drafting and revising stages are done with peer and teacher conferences, and drafts are kept in writing folders until students have a publishable piece. They then sign up to use WP in their classrooms, or, in the case of the intermediate grades and secondary school, the class might be scheduled into a computer lab to allow students to type in final copies. Software is now available to check spelling and even grammar and stylistic points. Called 'text editors', these programs are more apt to be found at secondary and adult levels.

The computer is an ideal tool to use when writing poetry. Students can play with line and space arrangements as they compose. The following poems were composed by fourth-graders using the Bank Street Writer, a very simple WP program that children learn easily:

The Sparkling Fields

The sun shines upon the fields of white,
Making them sparkle
As if they were sprayed with stars.

Laura Woodson

Medicine

Medicine in your mouth
Medicine in your tummy
Pink medicine for cherry-itis
Green medicine for greenpox
Red for strep strawberry
And Blue for blue flu.

Alyssa Winkler

Besides poetry and stories, children are using WP to write letters and publish newspapers. One fourth-grade in New Jersey combines letter-writing with learning about the world of computers as they write to people they read about (for example, the youthful founders of Apple Computers), asking how they became interested in technology. Since they write with WP, they almost always receive replies from these computer people who are impressed to see children using this new tool.

Producing a class or school newspaper is a perfect application for WP since articles can be typed in column form and thoroughly edited by peers or teacher-advisers before being printed. There are now specialised WP packages for just this purpose that include a graphics file and options to do banners and layout work.

Utility packages

Utility software provides teachers with frameworks for creating their own materials. It ranges from rather simple programs that permit the making of signs, crossword puzzles, wordfinds, and true/false or multiple-choice test items, to sophisticated authoring languages that allow teachers to write their own tutorial lessons. By just typing in a message and specifying size, you can print out classroom signs announcing birthdays, holidays and announcements in a matter of minutes. Teachers and children can create crosswords and wordfinds with vocabulary words from content area units. Recently, I saw a fifth-grader develop a crossword from words taken from *Twenty-One Balloons* by William Pene DuBois (1947). Having just finished reading this book, the class could be expected to be able to solve the puzzle.

Besides software that helps you create short answer tests in standard formats, there are programs that aid in the developing of cloze passages. The teacher can specify how often words or letters are to be deleted and then type in the passages; a tailor-made cloze procedure, based on text that you have selected, will be printed out.

Because highly developed authoring languages are now available, teachers do not have to know how to program to create their own computer-based lessons, simulations and problem-solving activities. Much more flexible than the utility programs described above, the authoring languages permit one to go beyond objective formats and design open-ended, interactive sequences that require students to respond in divergent ways. These systems now also have sound and graphic capabilities.

Readability software

Reading teachers and content area teachers often need an estimate of the readability, or difficulty level, of a text. Most readability formulas are based on the two variables of sentence length and word difficulty. According to the formulas, long sentences and words that are either unusual or lengthy are thought to make a text more difficult to read than text composed of short sentences and familiar, high-frequency words. While most formulas require the counting of sentences per 100 words to determine sentence length, some (Spache and Dale-Chall) count the number of words not on their high-frequency word lists and some (Fry and Flesch) count the number of syllables in a sample to determine word difficulty. These two quantitative figures are then entered into a formula to yield an estimate of reading difficulty, usually in descriptive terms or grade levels.

Assessing readability, with all this counting, searching of lists and calculating is a perfect application for a computer. Many programs, some yielding up to six different estimates to permit comparisons, are now available to teachers, who merely have to type in samples of passages from a text rather than to do the tedious work themselves.

While computerised readability assessment can be a valuable time-saving tool for teachers, it is wise to keep in mind the caveat cited by F. A. Dufflemeyer (1985) to 'beware the aura of precision' that is communicated. Just because a print-out shows a text to be at a specific difficulty level does not mean that all readers at that ability level will be able to read it with ease. Other concerns such as background knowledge and format/writing styles that are 'considerate' of readers (Armbruster, 1984) may be more important than a formula-derived level of difficulty. A readability estimate is really only one of many considerations to keep in mind when selecting texts for students. A. Davison (1984) says that the formulas consider factors that reflect difficulty rather than cause difficulty, pointing out that one of the main consequences of the formulas has been the rewriting or 'dumbing down' of texts as editors sometimes seek to use shorter sentences and words and unwittingly produce dull, boring texts written in unnatural language.

Despite the controversy, when readability formulas are used to estimate global levels, and these levels are just one factor to be considered by textbook search committees, they have some value. Having computer software to do the chore quantitative work frees teachers to look at the more important factors in the text and in the idealised readers for whom the texts are being selected.

Filing systems

Another computer tool that teachers can use to advantage is a filing system or simple database management system. Class files including standardised test scores, books read, interests and anecdotes can be created. Once you design a file (similar to designing a fill-in card file), you can enter information on all the children you teach. Information can be retrieved in many ways; for example, if you specify that you want to know which children were interested in 'animals', only those names would appear.

Book files can be created for the holdings in the class library. One teacher has developed a class book file to which students add comments after they read. They like reading what others have said about the book, and they prefer to type in their own responses rather than to write a formal book report. A reading clinic director has catalogued on disk all the 2000 trade books in his centre and can now quickly meet very specific requests. For example, a ten-year-old wanted to read mystery stories, so the director searched the file to see what mysteries, written on a beginner's level but at a higher interest level, were in the collection. In seconds he came up with five titles from which the boy could choose.

Students in a middle school in New Jersey used a computerised filing system to help them with two projects. One was an architectural study of historic houses in their community. Students interviewed owners of interesting older homes, taking notes on such information as dates they were built, materials used in construction, families who lived there and type of architecture. Later the information was entered into an electronic file; their pooled information created a database from which they could write. For example, one wrote on Dutch Colonial Homes from 1760 to 1800. Another group of students collected oral history from local senior citizens who had attended their school system. From a database of historical facts about their community, they wrote pieces on such topics as 'World War I Soldiers from our Valley' and 'Graduates of the Twenties Who Went to College'. There are almost no limits to the uses that teachers and students can make of easy-to-use filing/database software presently available to us.

The computer as tutor

As noted earlier, for teaching reading, the computer has been used mainly to deliver electronic drill and practice. Actually, the computer has the potential to be used in much more dynamic ways to develop reading strategies. Some interesting, whole text software is beginning to emerge, and some is still in the prototype stage.

Presently available is a program called 'The Puzzler', developed by Larry Miller and Dale Burnett of Queen's University, Canada, with educators from the Ontario and Scarborough school districts. Designed to develop predicting-confirming strategies, the program gives readers a screenful of text at a time and then asks them to make predictions about the main topic. They must make some predictions and type them in before they are permitted to continue reading. After the next screenful, they are permitted to delete, add or change their predictions, based on the information in the text.

One story, called 'Zingles', begins with the plea, 'Zing, there it goes again! Will people never stop rattling my brains?' It appears to be something found in shopping streets and supermarkets that people use all day long. The clue that a special noise accompanies its use prompts early predictions of *cash register*, *computer game*, and *sweet vendor*. The next sequence adds clues about size and use, '. . . little kids shake me repeatedly . . . watching my brains become fewer and fewer'. This usually causes readers to eliminate *cash register* and *computer game* (or others they may have made) and may elicit a new prediction, perhaps *chewing gum machine*. And so it goes on, with subsequent text either confirming some guesses and/or eliminating others until the story is finished.

Unlike the usual problem-solving exercises, no one 'correct' answer is given, to either students or teachers. The 'right' answer has to be the one most agree that the text supports. Although students may go through the program alone, it is recommended that they work in small groups so that they can discuss their predictions and cite support from the text. Having observed groups of three or four middle-grade children using the program, I can say that verbal interaction runs high.

A natural outgrowth of working through the stories on this

disk is to create 'puzzlers'. I have seen groups write some for the class to solve. These can be typed into a word-processor and formatted like the original, or presented on an overhead projector, section by section, with the class writing out their predictions.

J. Newman (1984) gives the program an excellent review, saying, ' "The Puzzler" ', then, emphasizes meaning rather than decoding or "comprehensive skills". It was constructed to support predicting, confirming, and integrating strategies for generating meaning.'

Dynamic books

L. D. and O. P. Geoffrion (1985) look forward to the availability of 'dynamic books' which would allow the reader to break free from the linear, sequential format of printed books. They say that leaving a text to look up a word in a dictionary or glossary or using a study guide to get through a complex novel disrupts the continuity of making meaning. Noting that even though non-linear previewing strategies such as SQ3R have been taught for years and few readers actually use them, they then make the case for computers:

> Computers, on the other hand, make extensive use of random-access devices. The computer can display any segment of information with almost instantaneous speed. Thus, a computer-based book can become a multi-dimensional learning environment where the reader can browse through the material according to personal goals and needs. The computer masks the intrusiveness of searching for material, by locating and displaying different portions automatically.
>
> (p. 10)

'Dynamic books', according to the Geoffrions, would permit readers to go quickly forward or backward in a text to search for a specific term, move 'upward' to an overview or to a 'command post' which would tell them where they were in a text, move 'inward' to pick up background information from an encyclopaedia or dictionary, move 'outside' by being able to take notes on a special electronic notepad, all the while never leaving the text, which can remain in view in a 'window' while the other pieces appear on the screen in separate 'windows'.

While this multidimensional text is not as yet available, the technology for it is here. The Apple Macintosh has a simple pointing device called a 'mouse' that moves the cursor around unobtrusively. The Geoffrions (1985) state, 'The elegant simplicity of the mouse pointer helps make the process of entering commands almost transparent to conscious attention' (p. 14). The Macintosh has 'windows' and 'pull-down menus' that offer the user many options to move around in a text.

As an example of how a 'dynamic book' or 'dynabook' would work, the Geoffrions present a page of text about reading readiness. At the top are the major options: OVERVIEW DEFINE NOTES EXPAND FILE HELP. At the bottom appear these direction options: BACK WHERE? NEXT. Reading along, one could get an overview of the next section, ask for a definition of a word, write some notes, get more information on something, go to a file, go back or forward in the text or ask where one was in the text.

If you came upon a reference to 'Sesame Street' and wanted to know more about it, you could highlight the term and call for the EXPAND option; a piece of text describing the television show would then appear in another window, thus supplying you with background information without your having to leave the text.

Prototypes of 'dynabooks'

Software containing some of the capabilities of 'dynabooks' have been appearing as experimental prototypes. D. P. Reinking (1983) noted many of the same differences between reading printed pages versus computer texts as did the Geoffrions. Accordingly, he applied some of the interactive characteristics of the computer to reading by developing a program which offered readers a number of options to help them understand a text. After reading a passage, students may request the meanings of certain words that are defined contextually. If they think the passage is too technical or too difficult, they can call for a version written at a lower readability level. If background knowledge is a problem, they can request more information. For example, for a passage on hailstones, an animated graphic showing how hailstones are formed appears. When students have difficulty following the structure of a text, they can ask that an outline be displayed. (This could also serve as an overview, as suggested by the Geoffrions.)

Since this tutor application of the computer also seeks to monitor comprehension and the strategies readers use, it keeps track of the number of times readers call for the various options and of the number of comprehension questions they answer correctly. If readers do not meet the criteria set for the passage, they may not go on but must reread the selection, again with the option of calling for help as needed. This record-keeping feature also makes the program an interesting research tool for monitoring reading behaviour.

Reinking (1984) has tested out his program as a comprehension enhancer with intermediate-grade students. Students reading his interactive text scored significantly higher on the comprehension questions than those reading the passages on the computer without the text-help options. He also found that readers will readily select the help options, especially the supplemental background information. Interestingly, consistently higher scores were achieved by one group of students who were required to read all the textual manipulations before selecting their own options. This led Reinking to conclude that computer control of the study habits of ten- and eleven-year-olds may be beneficial.

Other examples of unique tutor applications have been reported. G. W. McConkie (1983) studied illiterate adults as they worked with a computer-aided reading program that provided the pronunciation of unfamiliar words when they were touched on the screen with a light pen. It was observed that these adults appeared to learn to recognise many words in context this way since the same words were selected less frequently as they went through the text.

J. J. L'Allier (1980) developed a reading program that would lower the readability level of a passage if students took too long a time to read it and scored below a pre-set criterion on a comprehension check. Low-ability secondary school students who were channelled into the revised versions did as well as high-ability students reading the unrevised passages. The computer was able to match the text to the reader and enhance comprehension and learning.

These innovative uses of the computer as tutor, although only in research stages, demonstrate that the Geoffrions' (1985) 'dream of a dynamic book' is not far off. The computer can do more than offer drill and practice. It can set up optimum learning environments that permit learners to internalise reading strategies and gain meaning from print in whole language situations.

Conclusion

Computer hardware and software have come a long way in this decade and can serve as a valuable resources for teaching reading. Simple-to-use but powerful word-processing programs and software that can help teachers write programs, assess readability and develop databases with their students are all tool applications that are available now. Fast emerging are whole-text tutor applications in which the dynamic capabilities of the computer are being utilised. Software like 'The Puzzler' and Reinking's interactive comprehension program and hardware like the Macintosh herald a bright tomorrow for the role that computers can play in the teaching of reading.

References

ARMBRUSTER, B. B. (1984) 'The problem of inconsiderate text', in G. G. Duffy, L. A. Roehler, and J. Mason (eds) *Comprehension Instruction: Perspectives and Suggestions* (New York: Longmans).

CALKINS, L. (1983) *Lessons from a Child* (Exeter, New Hampshire: Heinemann).

DAVISON, A. (1984) 'Readability formulas and comprehension', in G. G. Duffy, L. R. Roehler, and J. Mason (eds) *Comprehension Instruction: Perspectives and Suggestions* (New York: Longmans).

DUBOIS, W. P. (1947) *Twenty-one Balloons*.

DUFFLEMEYER, F. A. (1985) 'Estimating readability formulas with a computer: Beware the aura of precision', *The Reading Teacher*, no. 38, pp. 392–5.

GEOFFRION, L. D. and GEOFFRION, O. P. (1985) *Beyond the electronic workbook* (Paper presented at the International Reading Association, New Orleans).

GRAVES, D. (1983) *Writing: Teachers and Children at Work* (Exeter: New Hampshire: Heinemann).

L'ALLIER, J. J. (1980) *An evaluation study of a computer-based lesson that adjusts reading level by monitoring on-task reader characteristics* (Unpublished doctoral dissertation, University of Minnesota).

McCONKIE, G. W. (1983) *Computer-aided reading: A Help for illiterate adults* (Paper presented at the annual meeting of the National Reading Conference, Austin, Texas).

NEWMAN, J. (1984) 'Online: Reading, writing, and computers', *Language Arts*, no. 61, pp. 758–63.

PHENIX, J. and HANNAN, E. (1984) 'Word processing in the grade one classroom', *Language Arts*, no. 61, pp. 804–12.

REINKING, D. P. (1983) *The effects of computer-mediated text and reader study behavior on measures of reading comprehension* (Unpublished doctoral dissertation, University of Minnesota.)

REINKING, D. P. (1984) *Reading Software: Current limitations and future potential* (Paper presented at the William Paterson College Reading and Computers Conference, Wayne, New Jersey).

RUBIN, A. and BRUCE, B. (1984) *Quill: Reading and writing with a microcomputer*, Reading Education Report no. 48 (Urbana, Illinois: Center for Study of Reading, The University of Illinois).

SMITH, C. B. (1985) 'How teachers use microcomputers for reading instruction', *California Reader* April/May, pp. 11–15.

Software

Bank Street Writer (Word Processing)
Scholastic Publications
730 Broadway
New York, NY 10003

(Apple, Atari)

MECC Readability
Minnesota Educational Computer Consortium (MECC)
3490 Lexington Avenue North
St. Paul, Minnesota 5512

(Apple)

The Puzzler
Sunburst Communications
Pleasantville, NY 10570

(Apple)

List of Contributors

Jonathan Anderson
Lecturer in Education
Flinders University
South Australia

Nancy Andrews
Reading Consultant
Maine Department of Educational
and Cultural Service, USA

Dr Roger Beard
School of Education
University of Leeds

Dr L. John Chapman
School of Education
The Open University

Dr Helen Cowie
Department of Education
University of Sheffield

Joan Dean
Chief Inspector
Surrey

Dr Viv Edwards
Lecturer
Birkbeck College

Dr Joan Feeley
William Paterson College
Wayne
New Jersey, USA

Professor Christian Gerhard
Department of Education
George Washington University
Washington, DC
USA

Professor Elizabeth Goodacre
Education Department
Middlesex Polytechnic

Ralph Lavender
Senior Primary Inspector
Essex

Sheila McCullagh
Author of Children's Books

Dr Joyce Morris
Reading Consultant and Author

Cliff Moon
Education Department
Bulmershe College of Higher
Education
Reading

Margaret L. Peters
Formerly Cambridge
Institute of Education

Angela Redfern
Deputy Head
Redlands Primary School
Reading

Betty Root
Tutor-in-Charge
Reading and Language Information
Centre
University of Reading

Rosemary Salesi
Associate Dean of Graduate School
University of Maine
USA

Sue Sheldon
School of Education
The Open University

Brigid Smith
Director of Communications Studies
Stewards School
Harlow

Professor Laura Smith
University of the District of
Columbia
Washington, DC
USA

Vera Southgate
Lecturer and Author
(Formerly School of Education
University of Manchester)